BALLYMONEY

An Illustrated History and Companion

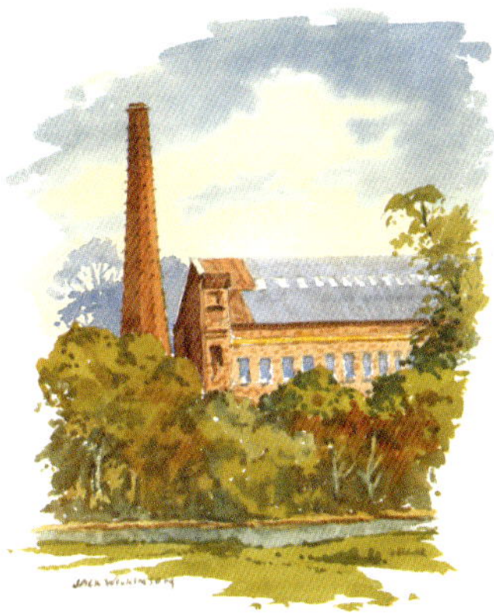

Paintings by

Jack Wilkinson

Text by

S. Alex Blair M.A.

Cottage Publications

First published by Cottage Publications,
Donaghadee N. Ireland 1995.

Printed in Singapore

ISBN 0 9516402 6 7

List of Contents

The Artist

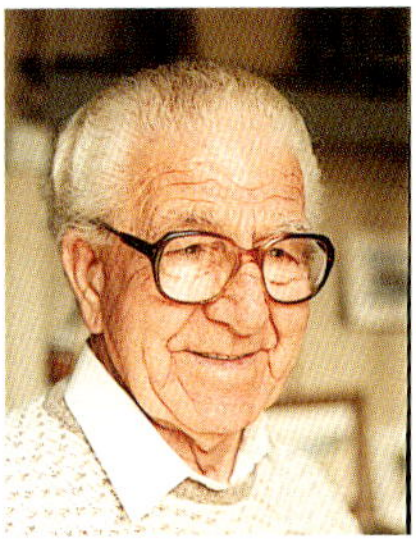

Jack Wilkinson has been painting in North Antrim for many years and, whether in water colours or oils, his work has a distinctive mood and style which has made it much sought after by discerning patrons across the province and beyond. He taught art in the technical colleges in Ballymoney and Portrush for 25 years and has also painted a number of portraits, most notably that of Ballymoney playwright, George Shiels, which hangs in the Gallery of the Abbey Theatre, Dublin. When not painting, Jack's other main hobby is singing and his fine bass voice has won many awards at music festivals over the last 50 years. He sings in St. Patrick's Church Choir, the Route Singers and is a founder member of Ballymoney and District Male Voice Choir.

The Author

Well known as 'the Historian of Ballymoney', S. Alex Blair has made a name for himself as a writer, lecturer and broadcaster. Author of eight books on local history, hailed as classics of their kind, Mr. Blair's lectures on the history of people and places in North Antrim always attract large audiences. He is Head of History and Senior Teacher at Dalriada School and plays a large part in the life of Ballymoney and District. He is secretary of the local drama festival and was, for many years, a Vice-President of the 'Young Farmers' Clubs Movement throughout Ulster, whose history he has written. A busy man who has travelled widely all over Europe, the Middle East and America, he lives at Kilraughts in the house in which he was born.

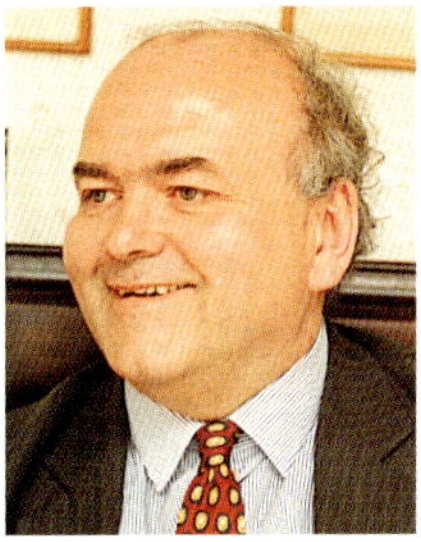

"Land of Promise"

The place-name Ballymoney is an anglicised version of two gaelic words which mean either 'the town in the shrubbery' or 'the town in the bog'. The latter is more likely to be correct as the nearby Garry Bog, much reduced today by drainage and cultivation, was the second largest in Ireland, and is still an important source of fuel for Ballymoney folk. The town is also known as 'the Capital of the Route', an historic designation going back to the 3rd century when a chieftain called Cairbre Riada took possession of much of North Antrim. Route is said to be a corruption of Riada and both names are used today for a number of business premises and public buildings such as the Route Hospital, the Riada Centre, Riada House and Dalriada School.

However, the history of the Ballymoney area goes back even beyond the 3rd century to the New Stone Age, when the first people came to Ireland. Many finds of flint axes from this period have been made and dolmens and standing stones in today's landscape are further reminders of those early times. One of the great burial cairns from the New Stone Age, known as Dooey's Cairn, still remains at Ballymacaldrick and another one at Enagh became the focal point for the development of fairs in Celtic times. This led to the town of Enagh Cross or the Crosses of Antrim, forerunner of Ballymoney, being established at a strategic crossing point on the River Bann where there was both a ford and a ferry.

It was the regional capital and seat of the local King or Ri, whose fortress was there. When Prince Murtough MacNeill of Aileach set out in 941 AD from Derry on a circuit of Ireland as a candidate for the High Kingship, Enagh Cross was his first stop. He and his entourage were greatly impressed by all they saw, as is evident in the flattering record of the visit made by his bard Cormachan. He described the area as "that land of promise" and wrote:–

> "We were a night at Enagh Cross
> Not more delightful to be in Paradise".

The Celtic Kings had elaborate ceremonies in which large trumpets were used, some over one and a half metres in length. They formed a kind of orchestra for royal occasions and eight of them have been discovered in the Ballymoney district, four at Drumabest, Kilraughts, and four in the Garry Bog. The Dalriada Brooch, dug up in a potato field at Enagh Cross in 1855, with elaborate decoration in gold, helps us to sense something more of the elegance of the Celts and especially of the life-style and dress of the dwellers in their 'Paradise' by the River Bann.

However the river was soon to prove their undoing. It provided easy access for raiders and in the 9th century, when the Vikings appeared, they brought terror to Enagh Cross. Subjected to frequent raids, it was natural that some inhabitants decided to move away to a safer position further back from the river, thus giving rise to the settlement of Ballymoney.

Ballymoney is not unique in having its origins some distance from its present site. Most old towns in Ireland follow this pattern. Before the influx of population from Enagh Cross in the 9th or 10th centuries, a small settlement already existed at Ballymoney. It was essentially a settlement gathered around two Celtic forts, one at the western end of what is now Castle Street and the other at the eastern end of what became in later years the lane to the meeting-house, now Meetinghouse Street. These provided the two main entrances to the town and when the Normans took over some centuries later, they erected a stone fortified house on or near the western fort. As such houses were often called castles, the street which developed took that name. The castle guarded the west gate of the town and the road to the Bann and to the old settlement at Enagh Cross, which still existed but only as a shadow of its former self. On the eastern fort-site a house stood for many years but was demolished in the middle of this century to facilitate road widening. It marked the southern entrance to the town and from these two entrances the basic street pattern of Ballymoney evolved. The roads from them converged in Main Street and continued to the Head of the Town and on towards Coleraine.

But to go back to the Celts: it was during their time that Christianity made its impact on Ireland and St. Patrick is said to have visited a number of places in the North Antrim area. At Dunseverick, on his last visit to the fortress there, he found the twelve sons of Erc, descendants of Cairbre Riada, quarrelling about the division of the Dalriadic Kingdom after their father's death. The youngest son, Fergus, was not given a part of the inheritance but Patrick intervened successfully on his behalf and prophesied that:–

> "Though thy brothers hath not much respect for thee today, it is thou that shall be King. The Kings of this country and over Fortrenn (Scotland) shall be from thee for ever."

Out of gratitude for his intervention, Fergus gave a portion of the territory he obtained to St. Patrick and there a church and monastery were erected. This was the seat of the first Christian bishop in Ireland. The place was Armoy and the bishop's name was Olcan. He had been discovered as an infant lying beside his dead mother at Drumbolcan (the ridge of Olcan) near Rasharkin by a local chieftain named Rory whose fortress was at Dunrory near the present village of Armoy.

Patrick's prophecy in regard to Fergus proved correct, for about 502 AD, with his two brothers Lorne and Angus, he invaded Argyle and the Scottish islands establishing himself as King of that area, which became Scottish Dalriada. From him were descended the Scottish Kings and Queen Elizabeth II is also of that same line.

When she visited Ballymoney on 3rd July 1953 a book was presented to her tracing her lineage back to the Dalriadic Kings. Also the coat of arms of the present borough of Ballymoney depicts royal coronets on the necks of the two supporting animals, indicating the local royal links.

A number of early churches and monastic foundations were established in other parts of North Antrim as well as at Armoy, most notably at Vow, Caldernagh near Dunloy, Kilraughts, Derrykeighan and at Ballymoney itself. The church there, by the 16th century, had expanded into an important complex of buildings, if one of the officials of the Lord Deputy Sussex is to be believed. He wrote:–

> "Also this day, 14th July 1556, we came to a Bishop's House
> which was with a castle and a church joined
> together in one, called Ballymoney."

A hundred years later the picture was very different. The Ulster Visitation Book of 1622 stated that the walls of the church of Ballymoney were "decayed and fallen to the ground". A similar kind of entry is to be found about most of the other early churches, and obviously the area needed a boost in population and a general rejuvenation. This was provided by the arrival of the Scottish planters.

Sir Randal MacDonnell, a member of a Scottish family who were Lords of the Isles, had gained possession of a large part of County Antrim from the McQuillans, including the entire Ballymoney area. He was confirmed in these lands in 1610 by his fellow Scot who had become King James I of England. Sir Randal then started private schemes of plantation by which he brought in Scottish settlers to work and stock the farms of his Antrim Estates. By the 1630s there were quite a few families – mostly lowland Scots – farming in the Ballymoney area and more joined them later on. The old ruined churches were repaired or rebuilt for these valuable new settlers who provided their landlord with good rents. A freestone slab in the tower of the old Ballymoney Church declares:–

> "This church was builded to ye Glory of
> God, 1637."

Also a letter written by Sir Randal to Archbishop Ussher of Armagh in 1631 stated that he had done his part to "carry out your instructions in the matter of repairing churches and have done several with the help of the clergy".

It must be remembered that although the Plantation effected much good to the economy of the area, it inflicted wrong on those who had been its inhabitants before the Planters came. These 'displaced Irish', as they were called, although not of any great numerical strength in the Ballymoney area, joined with others to show their resentment in what has come to be called the 1641 Rebellion.

The first news of this Rebellion to reach the Planters was when they heard that an Irish army was marching towards the ford at Portnaw, near Kilrea, to invade their territory. They were defenceless and their landlord, Randal MacDonnell, Second Earl of Antrim, showed no willingness to come to their aid. However, his agent, Archibald Stewart, who was residing at the Castle in Ballymoney, did what he could by raising an impromptu army which many of the Planters joined. They were able to block the Irish and prevent them crossing the Bann. Stewart's army was a collection of many groupings including a number of Scottish Highlanders led by the Earl of Antrim's cousin, Allister McColl MacDonnell, and a group of what were described as 'loyal Irish' under Tirlagh Oge O'Cahan. But these two groups and their leaders turned traitor on the others and massacred a number of them as they slept in their quarters at Portnaw. This opened the way for 'the Irish' to cross the Bann and get revenge on the Planters. One who was present took up the story:–

> "Allister McColl and Tirlagh Oge with all the whole Irish of the country, who after the murder did rise with them, with a great multitude of Irish officers who came over the Bann, marched unto James McColl MacDonnell's house at the Vow, near the Bannside, where they drew up their men. Thence the whole Irish, on both sides the Bann there present with their wives and children, fearing the remnant of Mr. Stewart's Regiment, kept together and marched into the Cross and set the town on fire and killed all the British (i.e. Planters) they could lay their hands on".

Some women and children of the Planters had taken refuge at the Cross and nearly all perished together with the men who defended them. Many years later forty skeletons, with skulls showing obvious signs of having been pierced by weapons, were dug up and were most likely the remains of some of those who perished in 1641.

The Planters who survived re-grouped under Stewart and a number of engagements followed. One of the biggest was at Leaney near Ballymoney where Stewart's forces were annihilated on what came to be called 'Black Friday', 11th February 1642. The town of Ballymoney was burned to the ground and Sir John Clotworthy in his *The Warr in Ireland from 1640 to 1652* tells how Stewart's men were charged "in the boggy ground" at Bendooragh and how that incident proved to be "a fatal break to the British in these parts".

The Planters were beaten and it took a Scottish army under General Munroe to restore peace and put them back into their farms again. For many years, it is said, they worked the land with a plough in one hand and a sword in the other.

In the period of the Commonwealth an army of Oliver Cromwell passed through the Finvoy area camping in a field adjacent to the Vow Old Graveyard. A Cromwellian officer, Captain John Galland, built a bawn or fortified farmhouse and yard adjacent to the Bann at what is now known as Moore Lodge, residence of Sir William Moore, Bart.

In 1660 the Restoration of King Charles II led to a more strict adherence to Episcopalianism and the Anglican prayer book in the churches where the Presbyterian planters worshipped. Ministers who refused to accept these changes were ejected and those ejected included the Rev. James Ker from the church in Ballymoney and the Rev. William Cuming from Kilraughts Church. The Planters rallied round these ministers and started building meeting-houses of their own. Thus the church unity which had existed was broken and the Presbyterians became a separate denomination.

In the stirring days of the Williamite Wars (1688-90) an Irish army under General Richard Hamilton quartered in the town for nearly a fortnight in March 1689 and when Schomberg arrived with his army to take up the cause of William III he billeted a number of his regiments for a time in the Ballymoney area. Donoy's Regiment stayed in Ballymoney, Finvoy and Rasharkin. Prince George's Danish Regiment of Foot were in Armoy, Billy and Derrykeighan, whilst the Jutland Danish Regiment had quarters in Loughgiel, Cloughmills and Clough.

The forces of James II were defeated at the Boyne in 1690 and even more decisively at Aughrim in 1691 and there followed a period when Penal Laws were enacted by the Irish parliament, dominated by the Anglican landed classes, against Roman Catholics and Presbyterians. Worship had to be held in secret and there were a number of places where, for example, the Catholics celebrated Mass. Ballymoney Catholics worshipped at Ballybrakes in the house of a Protestant named Hayes and in 'Neal Murphy's garden' where a large tree is said to have shaded the altar. There were penal altars in remote spots near Dunloy and Loughgiel and the Broad Stone at Finvoy was also used from time to time.

Over the years these laws were relaxed or ignored and the 18th century gradually developed as a time of new ideas when reform became a priority in the political and social spheres. The Presbyterians took the initiative here for, having accumulated some wealth, they wanted the vote and some influence on what was happening in their country. The Government did little to meet their demands and soon they came to the point where they decided force was the only weapon available to them. A young Dublin Protestant lawyer, Wolfe Tone, established the Society of United Irishmen in Belfast on 14th October 1791. Soon lodges of this organisation were formed in Ballymoney and in a number of other places in North Antrim. These were secret, oath-bound groups, plotting a rising, arming themselves with pikes and firearms if they could obtain them and drilling in fields at places like Derrykeighan and Kilraughts as well as in Ballymoney itself. Their commander in Co. Antrim was Henry Joy McCracken whose orders they awaited and on 6th June 1798 the orders came. They were to march to Antrim where the main battle was scheduled to take place. Led by Richard Caldwell of Harmony Hill, Balnamore, and John Gunning of Ballymoney, the Ballymoney United Irishmen marched to the hill of Kilraughts where they camped and were joined by a detachment from Derrykeighan led by Captain John Nevin and the local Kilraughts detachment. The whole force then proceeded southwards, linking up with men from Killymurris, Loughgiel and Clough and entered Ballymena where they captured the Market House. In Ballymena the news was relayed to them that the Battle of Antrim had gone ahead without them and that Henry Joy McCracken had been defeated. It was now a matter of getting home as quickly and unobtrusively as possible and that was not easy, for Ballymoney was sealed off by the Crown forces led by Lord Henry Murray. They searched the place and marked and burned 'rebel' houses. When those who had been away tried to get home, they were easily captured and court martialled. Others were hunted down as they tried to hide in various remote spots. The local magistrate, Mr. George Hutchinson, took responsibility for dealing with the rebels and he had a number hanged and many others were sentenced to transportation to America or Botany Bay or some such place. Two young men named Gamble and Caulfield were hanged at Ballymoney Town Clock, two others named Ballentine and Adams were hanged at Dungorbery Hill near Kilraughts and another young man, Samuel Dunlop, was hanged by the roadside at Pleasure Step near Bendooragh. Francis McKinlay of Conagher was hanged from a tree in front of St. Patrick's Church in Coleraine and his body was later buried in Derrykeighan Churchyard.

It took a long time for Ballymoney and District to recover from the traumas of 1798 and it coloured the thinking of many in the next century. The area became strong liberal territory and was in the forefront of the struggle for tenant right. Roman Catholic priests and Presbyterian ministers together with the tenant farmers themselves led this effort and one of the most colourful and eloquent of these clerics was the Rev. J.B. Armour, Presbyterian minister in Ballymoney. It was said that he "brought a tongue of fire to the cause". Tenant Right meetings were held in Ballymoney Town Hall and at one of these another cleric, the Rev. Dr. Nathaniel McAuley Brown of Drumachose, Limavady, articulated the tenants' demands as the 3 F's – Fair Rent, Fixety of Tenure and Free Sale – and this became the slogan of the campaign. W.E. Gladstone, the Liberal Prime Minister, granted these demands in 1881 and there followed the destruction of the old landlord-tenant system and schemes by which tenants 'bought-out' their land and became owner-occupiers. The Rev. J.B. Armour and a number of Liberals in the Ballymoney area supported Gladstone also in his efforts to introduce Home Rule for Ireland. They organised a famous meeting in Ballymoney Town Hall on 24th October 1913 to show Protestant support for the Home Rule cause and opposition to the Ulster Covenant and the

Unionist campaign which was being mounted by Sir Edward Carson. The meeting was not a success but the speakers, like the audience – all Protestants – included such personalities as Sir Roger Casement, Captain Jack White, son of the famous Field Marshal Sir George White V.C. of Broughshane and Mrs. J.R. Green, the historian from Trinity College, Dublin.

The 19th century brought many changes, not only in land ownership and politics, but in the economic life of Ballymoney and district. As well as that, the countryside was changed considerably and the shape of the town much altered by an Act of Parliament of 1837. This enabled the 'new line' to be cut from Ballymena through Ballymoney and on to Coleraine. The old road had gone through Dunloy and its landlord, George Hutchinson, greatly liked in Dunloy though much hated in Ballymoney, had tried to develop the place as a small town with new churches, a fair hill, a police barrack and also with a law court. Now the 'new line' by-passed Dunloy and the village became a backwater never having the opportunity to achieve the potential Hutchinson saw for it. The inn in the middle of the village where the horses on the mail coach had been changed and where travellers lodged the night closed down and a new inn was built at Killagan Cross. The new line passed over large areas of bogland and the idea of planting trees to enable the road to use their roots as a solid base proved successful and two series of fir trees at the Frosses have become landmarks along the road. The new line entered Ballymoney some distance east of the old road, necessitating a new bridge to be built over the Ballymoney Burn and connecting up with a small cluster of houses known, because of their position, as the Rodden Foot. It then ran through the middle of the Church of Ireland graveyard necessitating exhumation of many bodies, an event only possible because Sir Charles Lanyon, the surveyor for County Antrim in charge of building the road, was also the architect for the Representative Church Body. The new road then proceeded towards

Coleraine providing new streets later named Victoria and Charles and giving the town centre its first 'ring' road.

Not long after this another major development took place when the railway was inaugurated. The railway line to Portrush was opened in 1855 and stations were built at Dunloy and Ballymoney. In Ballymoney Seymour Street was created to enable 'the town to go down to the train' and named in honour of Hugh Seymour, 9th Earl of Antrim, who died in 1855 and was landlord of Ballymoney and chairman of the railway company. In 1880 a narrow gauge line from Ballymoney to Ballycastle was opened with stations at Dervock, Stranocum, Gracehill, Armoy and Capecastle. It remained a unique feature of travel in North Antrim until closure came in 1950.

Ballymoney was an elegant town in the 1790s with some fine Georgian houses. After the burnings of the 1798 period the town recovered in the 1830s and for the next forty or fifty years many new public buildings were erected including five churches, a new Court House and a new Town Hall, built by public subscription in 1866.

In 1835 Thomas McElderry from Leitrim, who had been weighmaster for the Earl of Antrim, purchased a lease giving him the right to collect tolls on goods and operate markets in Ballymoney. Mr. McElderry changed the whole pattern of marketing in the town by introducing the new idea of market yards for the sale of the different products including grain, butter, pork and poultry. In October 1864 a new fair hill was set up off Meetinghouse Street for the sale of cattle, pigs and sheep and it was made clear that from then on no livestock was to be "exposed for sale or kept standing on any of the public streets of the town".

Ballymoney rapidly expanded as a market town and was especially famous for its cattle. The bridge over which many of them were driven 'on the hoof' into market was called "the Cow Bridge" and the town itself has often been referred to as "cow town".

Linen and the production of flax were also features of the area. In 1837 Samuel Lewis reported about Ballymoney:

> "The linen market has been long established and is eminent for the superior quality of the goods sold. From 15,000 to 20,000 double pieces are annually sold and on the first Thursday in every month large quantities of seven-eighths linen of various qualities are sold here, principally for the London market."

Flax was a major cash crop in the rural areas. In the 1864-5 season 1 437 tons of scutched flax were marketed in Ballymoney and the market remained buoyant until after the Second World War when it declined. In the 1944/5 season Ballymoney still provided an annual total of 1 444 tons of scutched flax and many flax mills still existed all over North Antrim.

The 20th century brought much expansion to Ballymoney with new houses being built and the town became noted for its schools and hospital facilities. In 1933 the American millionaire Samuel Robinson of Philadelphia, a native of Culcrum, Cloughmills, erected the Robinson Memorial Hospital in memory of his parents.

Ballymoney has also become well-known as a cultural centre. Its Drama Festival, founded in 1934, is the oldest one in Ireland still operating annually. George Shiels, the distinguished Irish playwright wrote most of his famous plays during the 1920s and 1930s in his home in Main Street, basing them on local people and using local situations and settings. In March 1981, the centenary of the playwright's birth, the Drama Festival erected a bronze mural relief sculpture by Angela, Countess of Antrim, in Ballymoney Town Hall to commemorate George Shiels. In the local grammar school, Dalriada School, Mr. Edmund Gordon produced a Shakespeare play each

December for thirty two years (1942-1974) and one who took part in some of these productions wrote that they:–

> "..brought enjoyment of Shakespeare to many who would otherwise not have found it and for those more intimately involved a taste for the theatre which we have never lost."

Music, literary and debating societies as well as drama groups, Irish dancing and traditional music groups and two well-known choirs are other aspects of a rich cultural scene in Ballymoney and district.

In the recreational field the town is also well-known. Another plaque in the Town Hall commemorates Kennedy K. McArthur from Dervock who won the Marathon Race at the Olympic Games in Stockholm in 1912. In more recent days the town opened in 1981 the Riada Centre, one of the leading leisure and sports facilities in the province and there is also at Ballybrakes Business Park an Indoor Bowling Stadium comprising eight full-sized rinks of international standard. Drumaheglis Marina and Caravan Park on the side of the Bann is a most attractive facility and the Leslie Hill Heritage Farm provides a link combining culture, history and recreation.

Ballymoney became a borough in 1977 and its armorial bearings were designed by Windsor, Herald of Arms, and granted by letters patent, dated 16th January 1979. The motto of the borough is 'Goodwill to all people'. Although the population of this rural borough is now around 25000, it is still a homely place to live, where people know each other and mix well in a spirit of neighbourliness and goodwill. The declaration of part of the town as a conservation area in 1994 has heightened the people's awareness of their rich history and their desire to preserve the best of it for future generations.

Important dates in Ballymoney's History

3000 B.C. Date given to grain of corn found at Dooey's Cairn.

460 A.D. St. Colman established a church at Derrykeighan.

1262 Rents of the Norman Manor of Lissanoure amounted to £65 7s 10d, the highest in Twescard.

1556 Earl of Sussex, Lord Deputy of Ireland, visited Ballymoney.

1641 Ballymoney burned.

1642 Battles of Leaney and Bendooragh.

1674 William Leslie acquired Clough Corr or Prospect and established a fortified house there.

1733 George Macartney, Sovereign of Belfast, purchased the Lissanoure Estate.

1742 George Macartney purchased the Dervock Estate.

1775 Ballymoney Market House (now Masonic Hall) built.

1785 John Wesley preached in Ballymoney Market House.

1792 United Irishmen met in Ballymoney to celebrate the Fall of the Bastille.

1797 Hugh Montgomery, whose family founded what became the Northern Bank, purchased the Benvarden Estate.

1798 United Irishmen's Rebellion.

1813 Erasmus Smith Free School opened in Ballymoney.

1826 Pyper Row renamed Charlotte Street.

1827 Medical Dispensary established in Ballymoney.

1834 Two arches of Stranocum Bridge swept away in great flood.

1843 Ballymoney Poor House opened.

1845 Ballymoney Town Commissioners established.

1847 Lissanoure Castle destroyed in accidental explosion.

1850 Ballymoney streets first lit by gas.

1856 Model School and Model Farm set up.

1869 Route Tenant Right Association formed.

1878 Intermediate School (now Dalriada School) founded.

1883 Body of United Irishman, Alexander Gamble, uncovered at the Diamond.

1896 William McKinley, whose ancestors came from Conagher, elected 25th President of USA.

1898 Urban and Rural District Councils established for Ballymoney area.

1906 Technical Institute, Charles Street, opened by the Lord Lieutenant of Ireland, the Earl of Aberdeen.

1917 Cardinal Cahal Daly born at Ballybradden, Loughgiel.

1933 Robinson Memorial Hospital opened.

1935 Professor E. Estyn Evans excavated Dooey's Cairn.

1937 Route Hospital opened in renovated Poor House premises.

1953 The Queen and the Duke of Edinburgh visited Ballymoney.

1959 Balnamore Mill closed.

1977 Ballymoney granted borough status.

1979 Mayoral chain presented to Mayor of Ballymoney.

1981 Riada Centre opened at Garryduff Road.

1993 Joey Dunlop, Culduff, world champion racing motor cyclist, made a freeman of Borough of Ballymoney.

1994 Part of Ballymoney declared a Conservation Area.

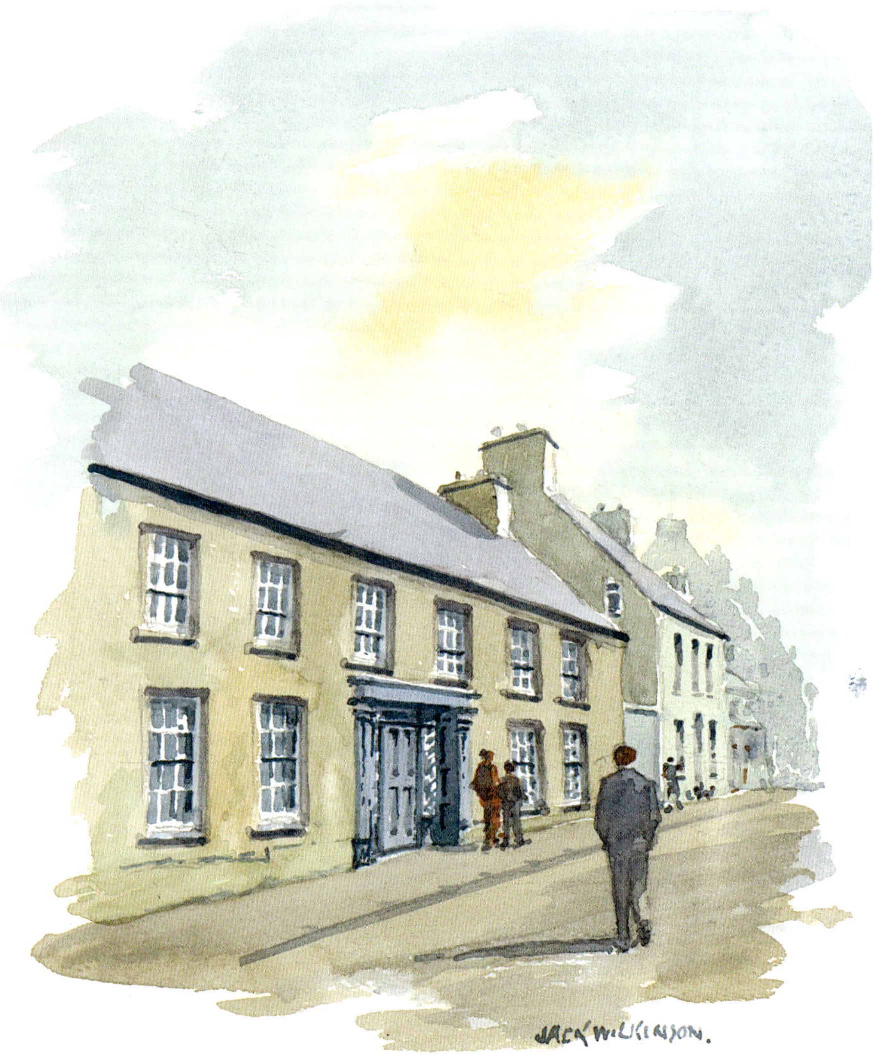
JACK WILKINSON.

Name and Address | *Telephone*

Name and Address	Telephone

CHARLOTTE STREET

Two of the many fine Georgian houses in Charlotte Street, Ballymoney. These houses have good windows, their original shutters and elaborate doorcases, one with sidelights and overlight, the other with fanlight. The house on the right accommodated Ballymoney's first bank and at the side is a gateway leading to a well-preserved coach house. Gateways were not usual in Ballymoney, for in the 1832 Ordnance Survey Memoir it is reported that cows and horses kept in yards often had to pass "to their stables either through halls or kitchens". The house on the right is now Ballymoney Heritage Centre where museum displays and exhibitions of various kinds are mounted regularly.

With thanks to The Winsome Lady

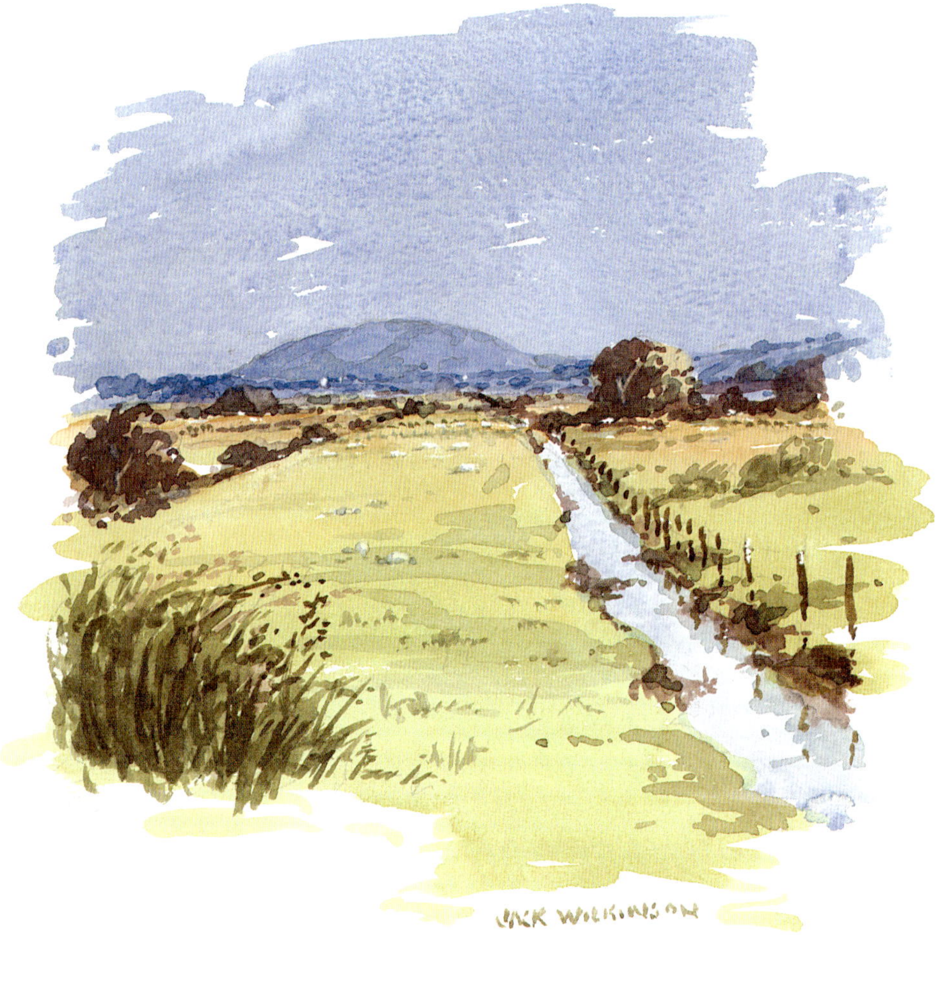
JACK WILKINSON

B

Name and Address	*Telephone*

THE GARRY BOG

These extensive boglands once formed the second largest peat bog in Ireland. Although much of it has been drained and cultivated, a substantial amount still remains in its original state. Many archaeological finds have been made here including four Bronze Age trumpets and the area is famous for its flora and fauna. Often called "the Holland of North Antrim" because it is so flat, it may be easily seen from the roads leading either to Portrush or Dervock. The Garry Bog provides peat for the fires of many homes in Ballymoney and district and quantities of bog fir are also found.

With thanks to Gossoon's Wine Bar / The Parklight Restaurant

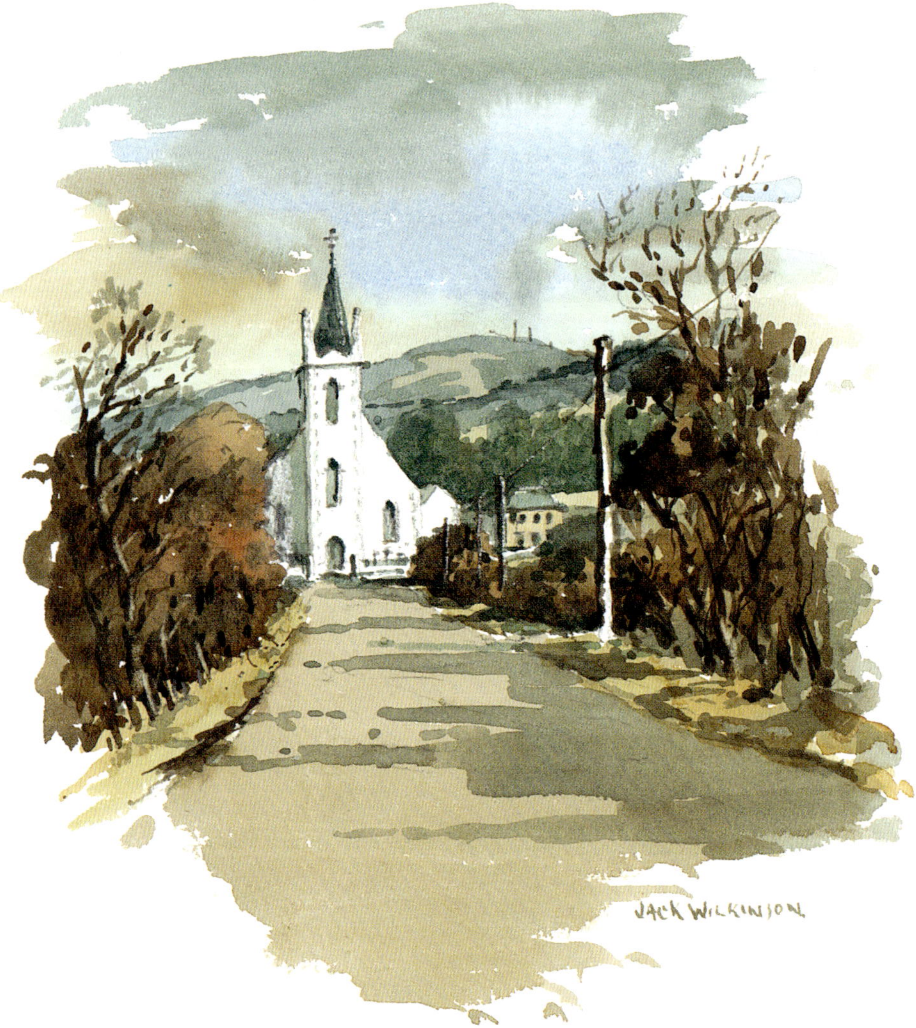
JACK WILKINSON

C

Name and Address	*Telephone*

St. Patrick's Church, Loughgiel

There had been a "Mass House" in the Lissanoure estate for many years but in 1786 Lord Macartney persuaded the parish priest to accept a site for a new chapel outside the demesne and surrender the old site. This was agreed but Macartney inserted in the lease a clause which said that he could cancel it at any time if he paid the priest £210. George Hume Macartney did this and dispossessed the Catholics of their church. They built their new church in 1839 on an elevated site on land bought from the Whitla family from Belfast to "look down on Macartney for ever"! The graveyard contains the graves of the parents of Cardinal Cahal Daly, who was brought up in the parish.

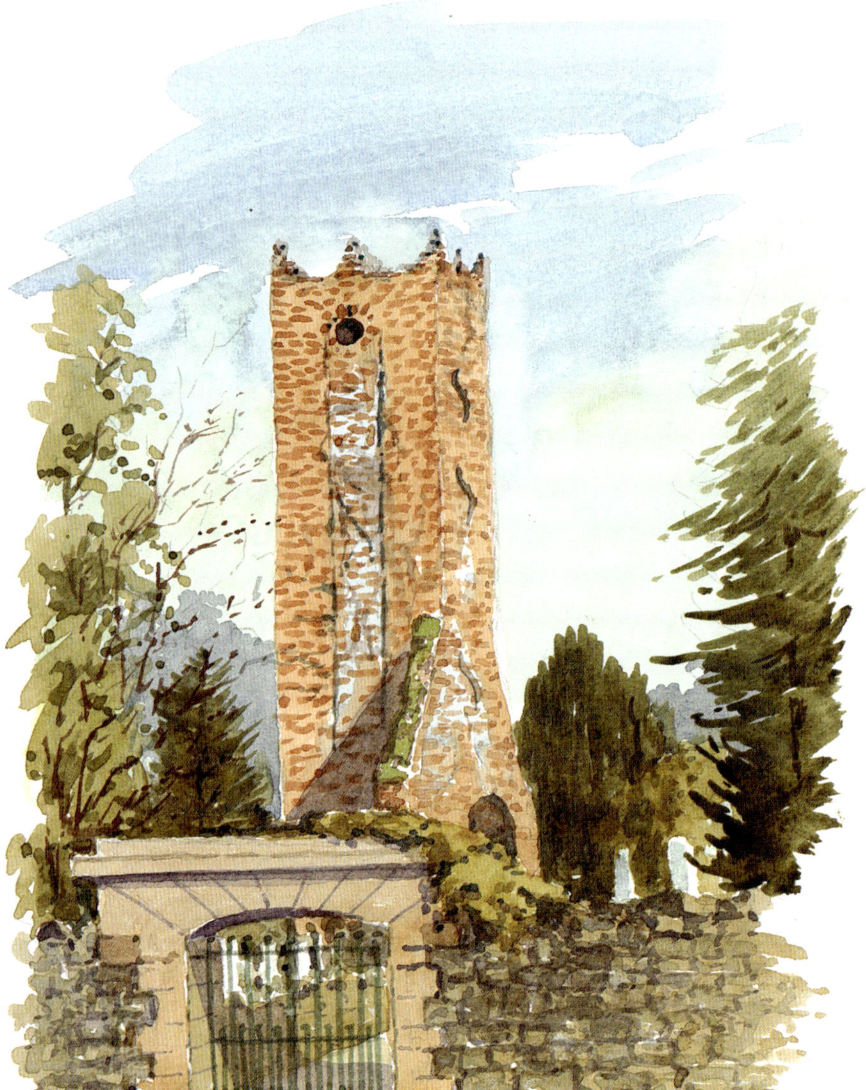
JACK. WILKINSON.

D

Name and Address	*Telephone*

THE OLD CHURCH TOWER, BALLYMONEY

The Old Church Tower is the oldest extant building in the town. It is all that remains of a church built in 1637, burned in 1641 and rebuilt and used until 1782. The surrounding churchyard contains many interesting tombs including those of Alexander Gamble, United Irishman, whose body was unearthed at the Diamond in 1883, George Hutchinson, the magistrate who was responsible for putting him to death, and an ancient Camac headstone built into the wall when the 'new line' was cut through the graveyard in the 1840's resulting in exhumation of many bodies.

With thanks to Ballymoney Borough Council

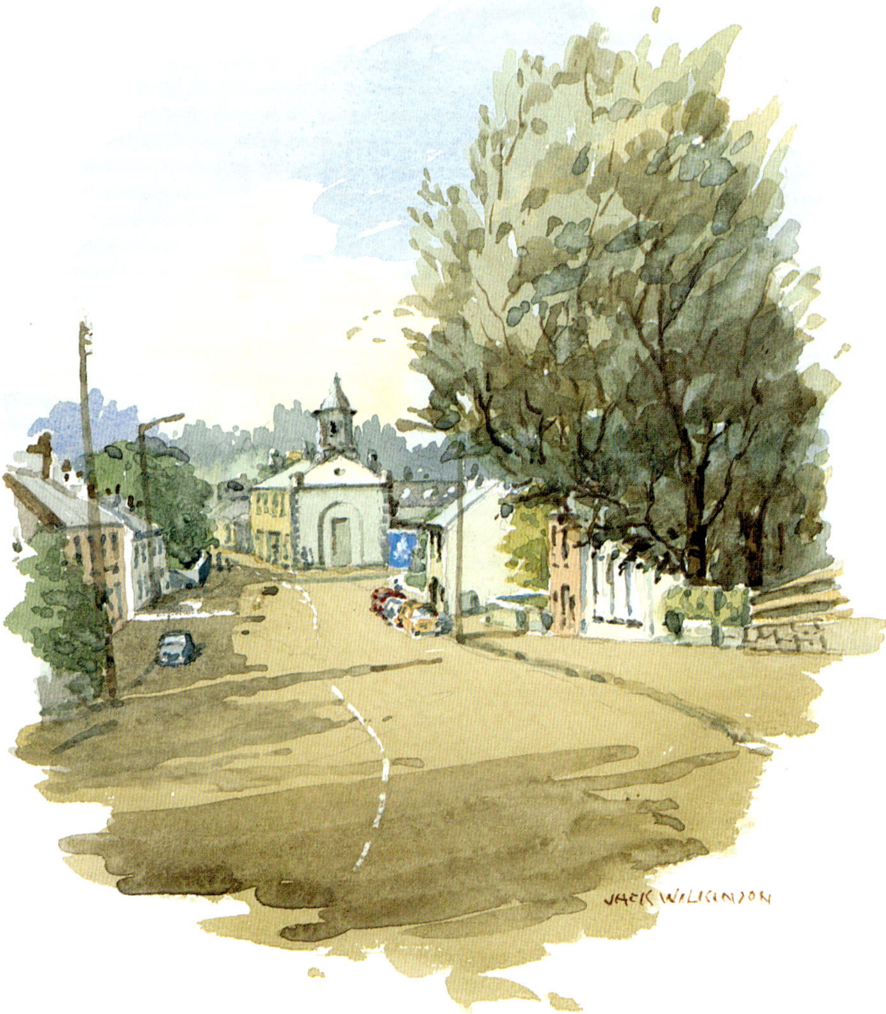
JACK WILKINSON

E

Name and Address	*Telephone*

Dervock Village

Dervock Village was the centre-piece of the Dervock Estate purchased by George Macartney in 1742. His grandson, Earl Macartney, British Ambassador to Russia and China and Governor of the Cape, took a special interest in the place and was responsible for having a Market House built in 1805 with a belfry, as well as many other houses and a school. He was followed by George Hume Macartney who was said to have "destroyed more than the Earl built" and let the houses fall into disrepair. However his successor, George Travers Macartney, redeemed the family image by being a good landlord and when he died in 1874 a fountain was erected to his memory.

With thanks to Old Ballyness Cottages, Bushmills

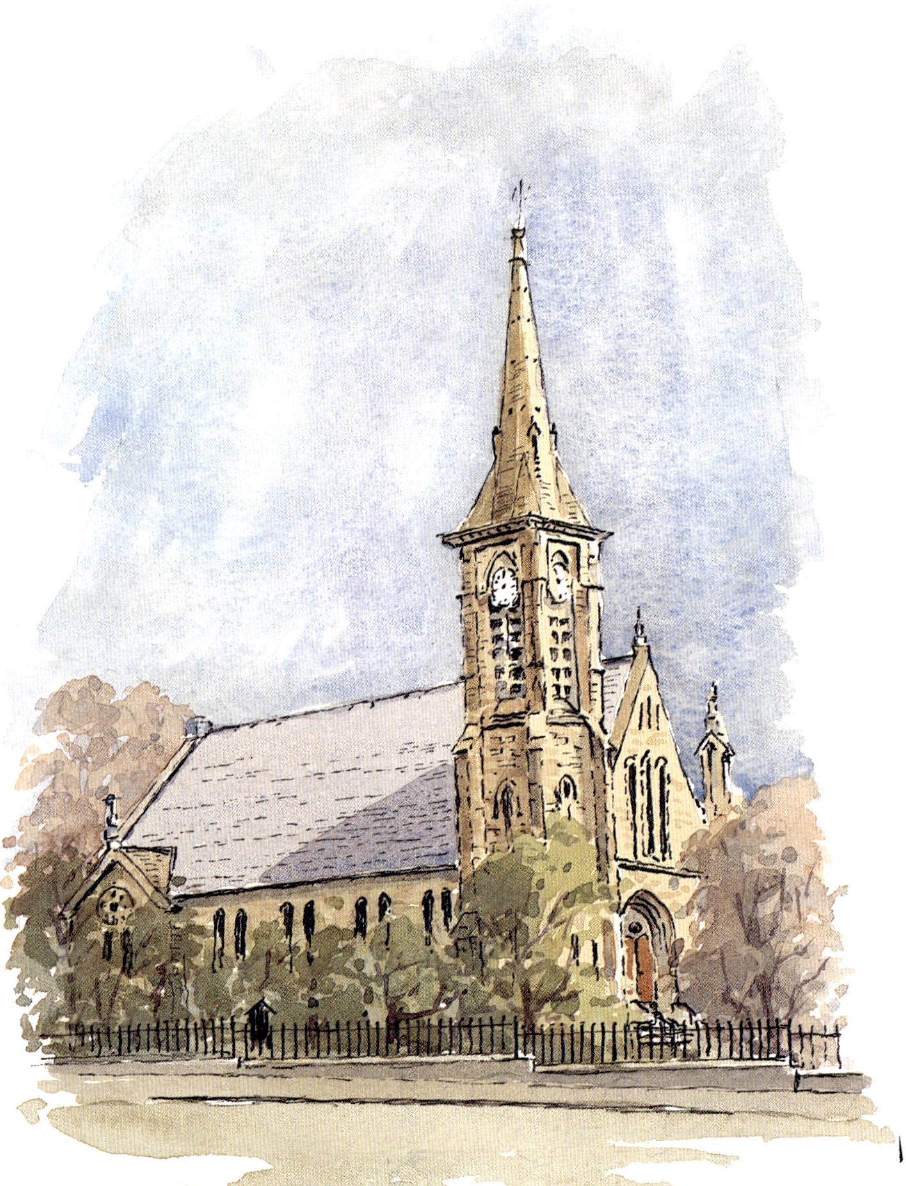
JACK WILKINSON

F

Name and Address	*Telephone*

TRINITY PRESBYTERIAN CHURCH, BALLYMONEY

Opened in 1885 by the Rev. Dr. John Hall of New York, Trinity Church began as a Seceder Society in Pyper Row. Later a disused malt kiln at the Roddenfoot was acquired. The minister in 1885 was the Rev. J.B. Armour and the building is still often called 'Armour's Meetinghouse'. The fact that it had a tower and spire was regarded as radical for Presbyterian churches at that time and it was said that when Armour was a candidate for a professorial chair at Magee College, this was held against him and he was not appointed. He became a leader in the Tenant Right Campaign and later a supporter of Home Rule, a very controversial stance in the Presbyterian Church of the time.

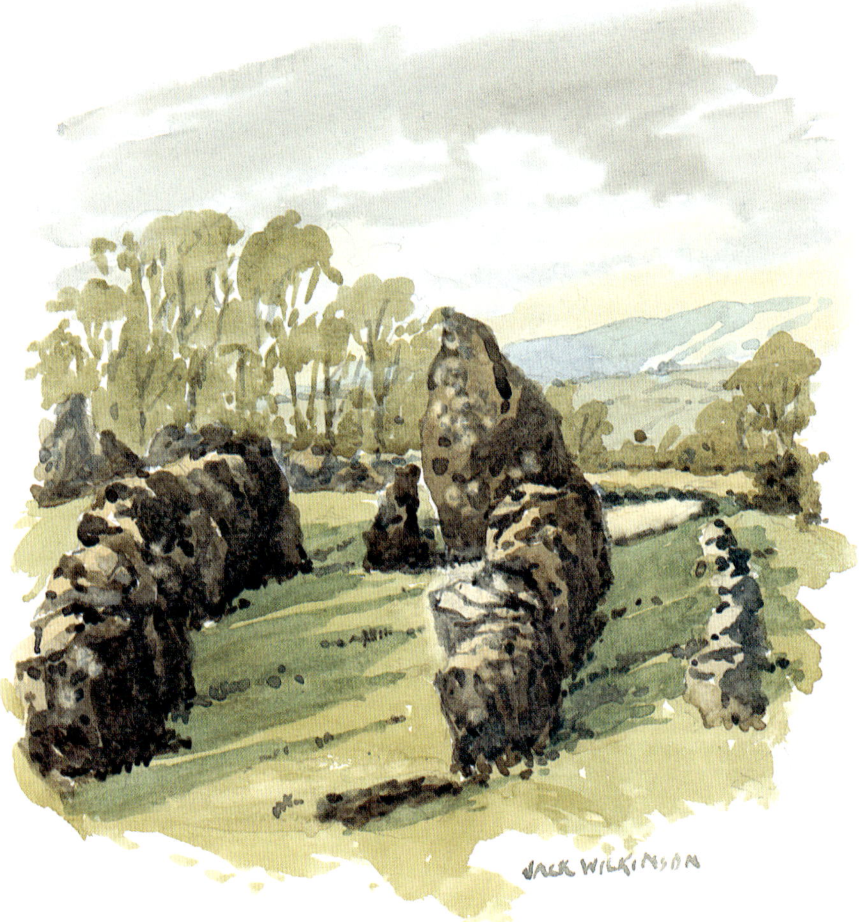
JACK WILKINSON

G

Name and Address	*Telephone*

Dooey's Cairn

Dooey's Cairn, Ballymacaldrick, Dunloy, is named after Mr. Andy Dooey, antiquarian, poet and Gaelic scholar, on whose land it stood and who was instrumental in having it excavated by Professor E. Estyn Evans in May 1935. It is an excellent example of a court cairn of the horned variety from the New Stone Age. It has three parts – a forecourt, a burial chamber and a cremation passage. Pots, flints, arrowheads, beads and parts of teeth of sheep and oxen were found in the burial chamber and one of the three pits in the cremation passage showed much evidence of use. In 1975 the Dooey family handed over the monument to state charge.

With thanks to S. Dooey & Co.

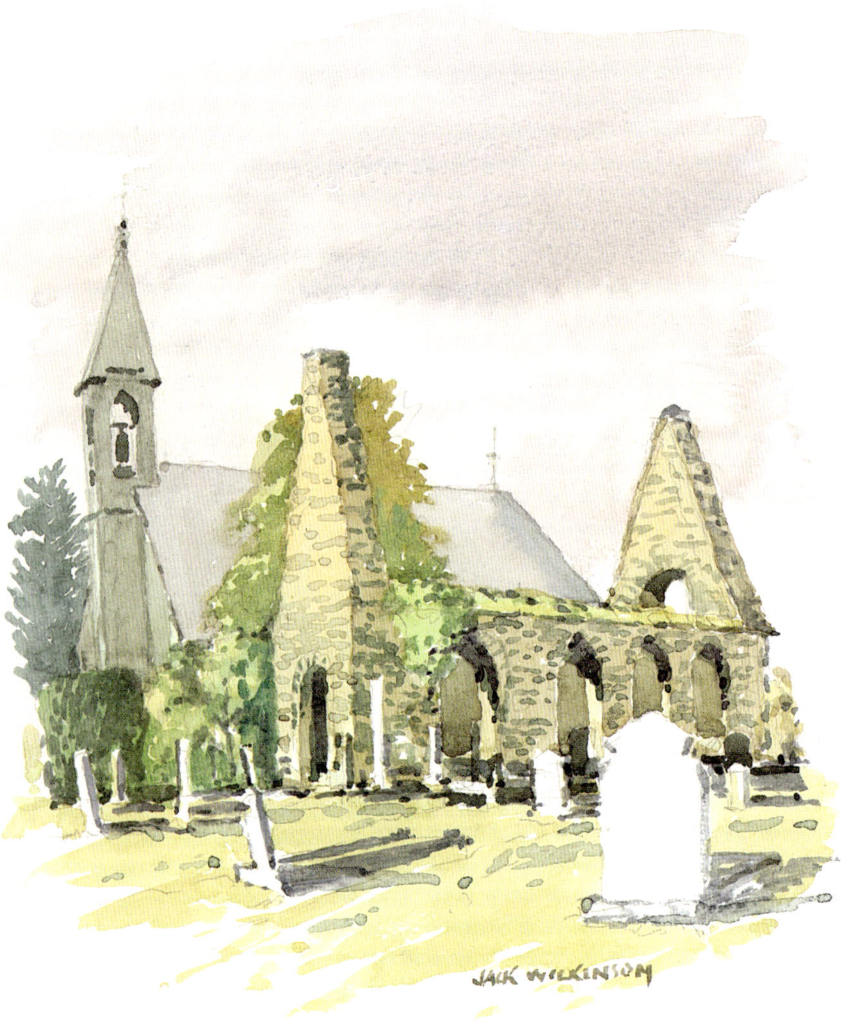
JACK WILKINSON

H

Name and Address	*Telephone*

ST. ANDREW'S CHURCH OF IRELAND, RASHARKIN

St. Andrew's was built in 1868 beside the remains of a much earlier church, dedicated to St. Olcan, who was discovered as a weeping infant beside his dead mother at nearby Drumbolcan. He was created the first Irish bishop by St. Patrick at Dunseverick. There has probably been a church on this site since the 5th century but the present ruins date from the 17th century. A tradition states that during the 1641 Rebellion a number of Planters took refuge in this old church and they and it were burned by the 'displaced Irish'. The old church was described by Lewis in his 'Topographical Dictionary' as "small but very beautiful".

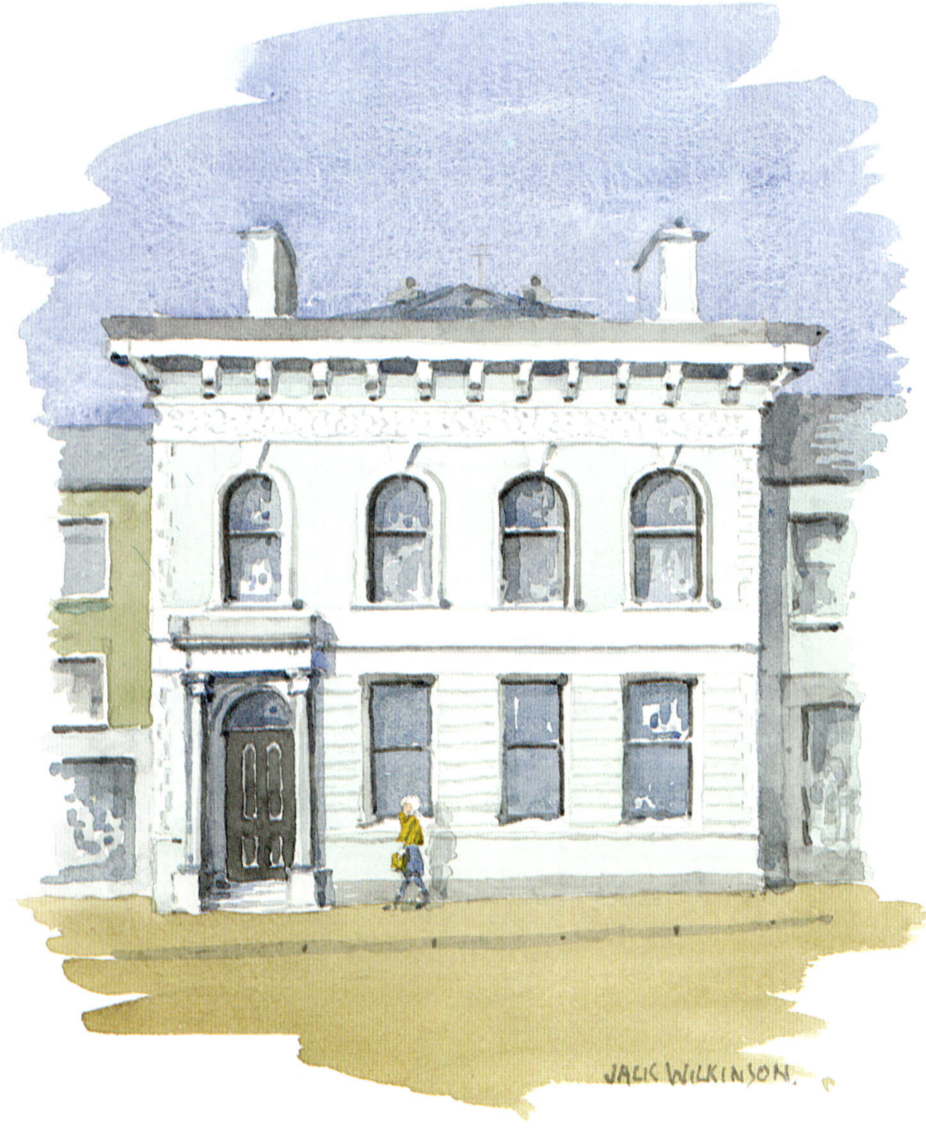
JACK WILKINSON.

I

Name and Address	*Telephone*

NORTHERN BANK HOUSE, BALLYMONEY

This fine building was built by the Earl of Antrim about 1760 as a ballroom and assembly room for the gentry during visits to the races and other events organised at least twice a year by the Antrim Hunt whose headquarters were in Ballymoney. One rule of the Hunt was that 'balls are to be three times a week or oftener, if the ladies please'. Invasion by France seemed a real threat in the 1780s and 90s and arms were stored in this building. The arms were removed in 1793 when the building became a barrack for dragoons. In the 1830s the building was leased to Mr. James Cramsie and in 1850 the front room became Ballymoney's first public library and news room.

With thanks to Northern Bank Limited

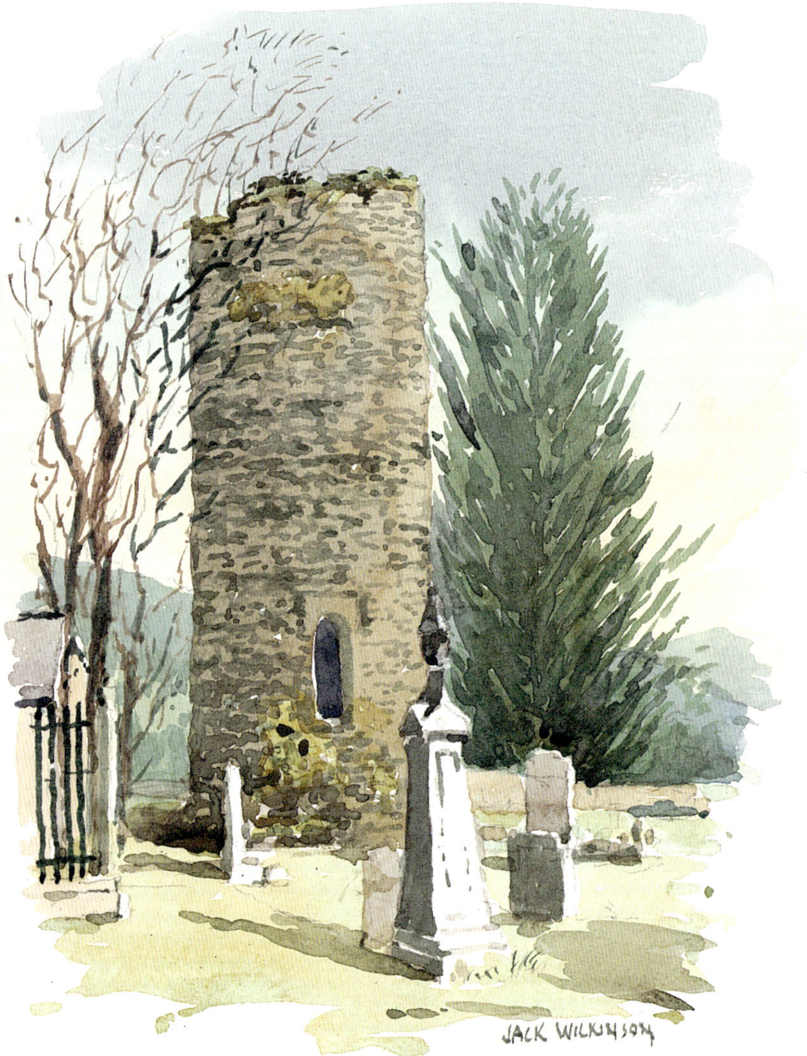
JACK WILKINSON

J

Name and Address	*Telephone*

Round Tower at Armoy

This stump is all that remains of a monastic complex of buildings which existed at Armoy from Celtic times. Round towers were built as protection against the Viking raiders who came to Ireland in the 9th and 10th centuries and raided wealthy and important places like Armoy. Sometimes they were also used in quieter times as belfries. There were a number of floors inside with ladders giving access from floor to floor. The door of Armoy Round Tower is very narrow so that it has often been said the Armoy monks were poorly fed and the thinnest monks in Ireland! In 1805 an attempt was made to pull down the tower but this was resisted and the stump has survived.

With thanks to J.S.C. Builders Merchants

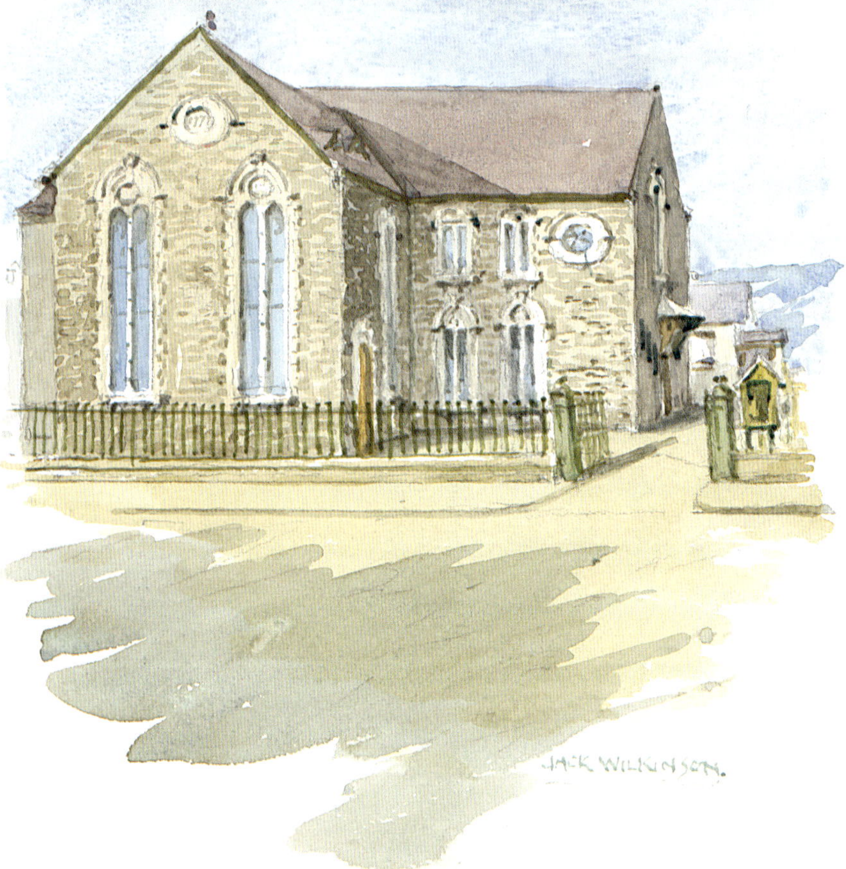
JACK WILKINSON.

K

Name and Address	*Telephone*

Ballymoney First Presbyterian Church

First Presbyterian Church, Meetinghouse Street, Ballymoney, is the oldest church building in the town. It was built as a rectangular barn church in 1777 and contains an ancient chair from an even earlier meetinghouse which stood on an adjacent site. A transept was added in 1871 and the interior of the building was considerably altered in 1921 when a new organ was installed. Often called "the cathedral of Presbyterianism in the Route" it is an impressive building with a great beamed roof. The east window contains the coats of arms of the regiments in which members fought in the First World War and the borough's annual Remembrance Day Service is held in the church.

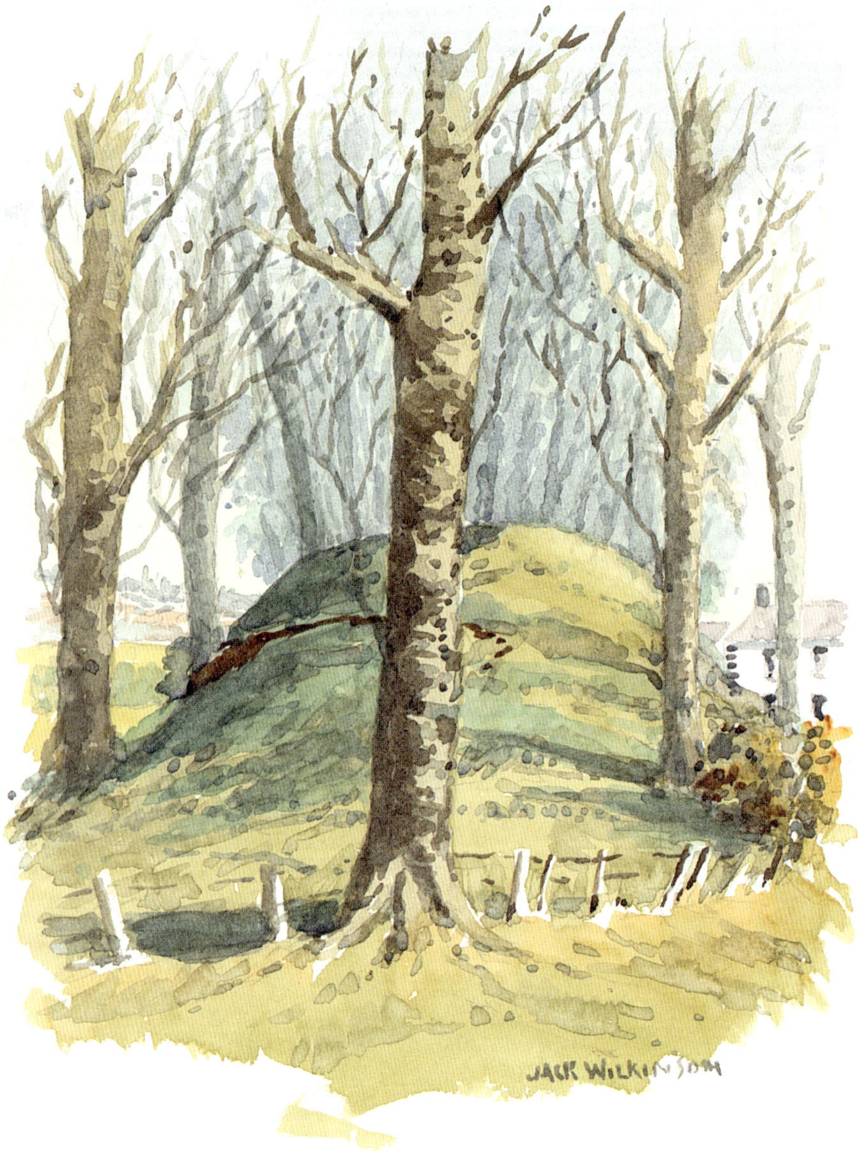
JACK WILKINSON

L

Name and Address	*Telephone*

Celtic Fort at Drumart

In an Inquisition of 1333 Drumart is included as one of the townlands in the Norman Earldom of Ulster. When the Scottish MacDonnells took possession of North Antrim at the beginning of the 17th century the Route was subdivided into nine tuoghs, one of which was Ballymoney and Drumart. An impressive Celtic ring fort stands in the townland, by the side of the Kirk Road, with a commanding view of the surrounding countryside and the town of Ballymoney. These forts were farmsteads in Celtic times and beside the fort stands the farmhouse of today, which links this place with the farming industry for at least fifteen hundred years!

With thanks to Top Ten

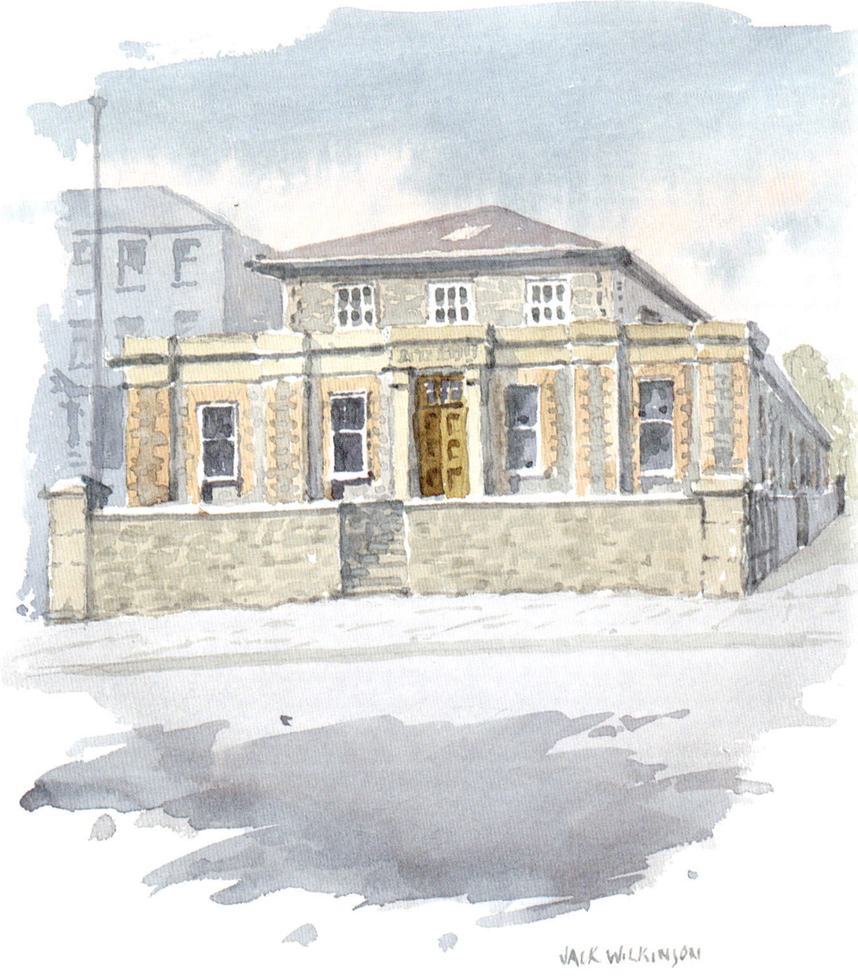
JACK WILKINSON

M

Name and Address	*Telephone*

Ballymoney Court House

The Court House is said to have been the apprenticeship work of the famous Ulster architect, Sir Charles Lanyon. It was built about 1838 when the court was transferred from the old Court House in 'the Diamond'. An unusual feature is the vitruvian doorway which gives the building more semblance of height. The ground floor was the main courtroom with the smaller upper room used for juvenile and special courts. In a small ante-room is a memorial to Lieutenant J. Kenneth M. Greer, son of Senator T.M. Greer of Westoncrofts, who was an apprentice solicitor and was killed at the Battle of the Somme, 1916.

With thanks to Murphy Irwin & Co.

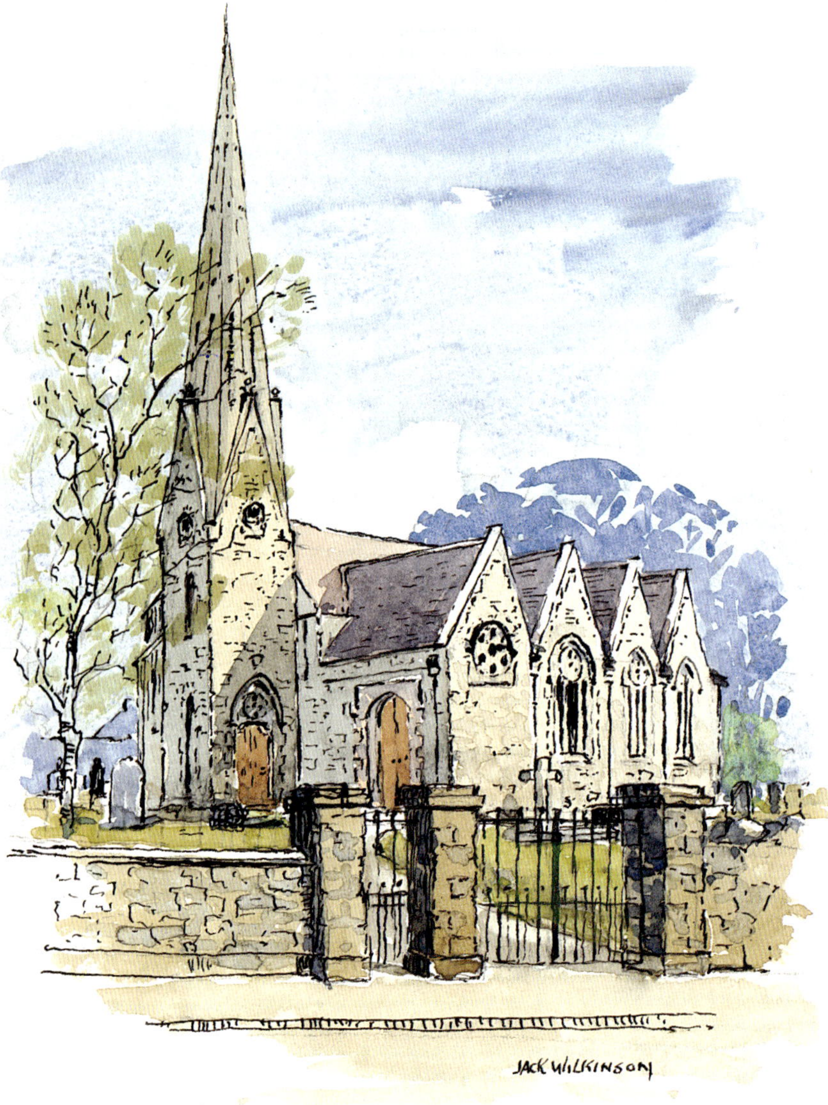
JACK WILKINSON

Mc

Name and Address	*Telephone*

St. Patrick's Church of Ireland, Ballymoney

St. Patrick's assumed its present shape as the result of renovations and additions made in 1867-8. The original church on the site was built in 1782 and replaced an old church, the tower of which still remains in the Old Churchyard. The building contains many memorials including one to the Rev. Robert McBride, Presbyterian minister in Ballymoney and there is a Celtic Cross in silver, a memorial to a former rector, the Rev. Canon J.T. Armstrong (rector 1925-59) the historian of Dalriada. A rear screen commemorates another rector, the Rev. J.R. Phillott whose wife published 'The Rectory Garden and other Poems' in 1866.

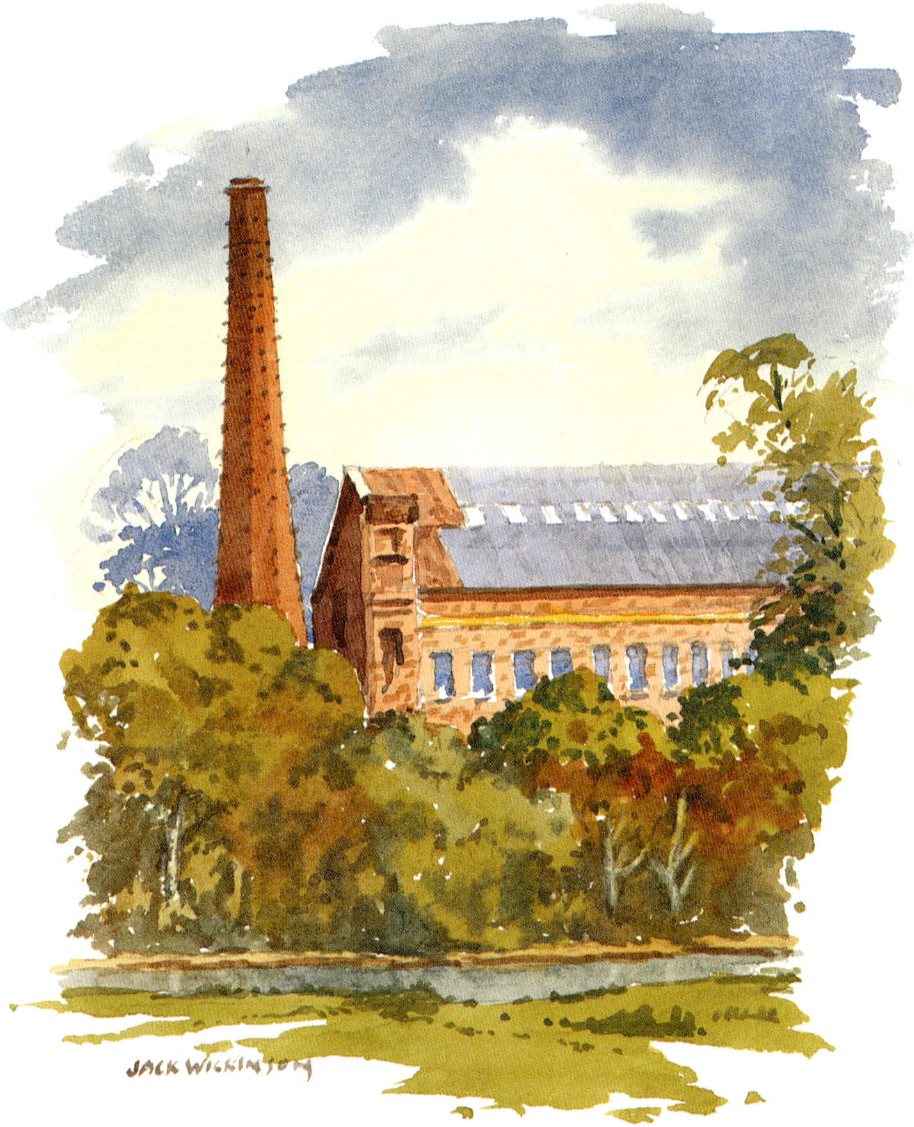
JACK WILKINSON

N

Name and Address	*Telephone*

Balnamore Mill

Balnamore Mill closed down in February 1959 after a century and a half of production. In 1790 the Caldwell family had a corn mill and bleach green here but they had to flee to America because their son was a leader in the United Irishmen's Rebellion of 1798. John Bryans purchased the place in 1809 and started a spinning mill which was subsequently improved and enlarged by Thompson Bryans. The mill's most prosperous period was when it was owned by the Braidwater Spinning Company from about 1880 until 1920. The mill village, a few yards from the mill, had three streets, Front Street, Back Street and the Ark.

With thanks to The Nature Nook

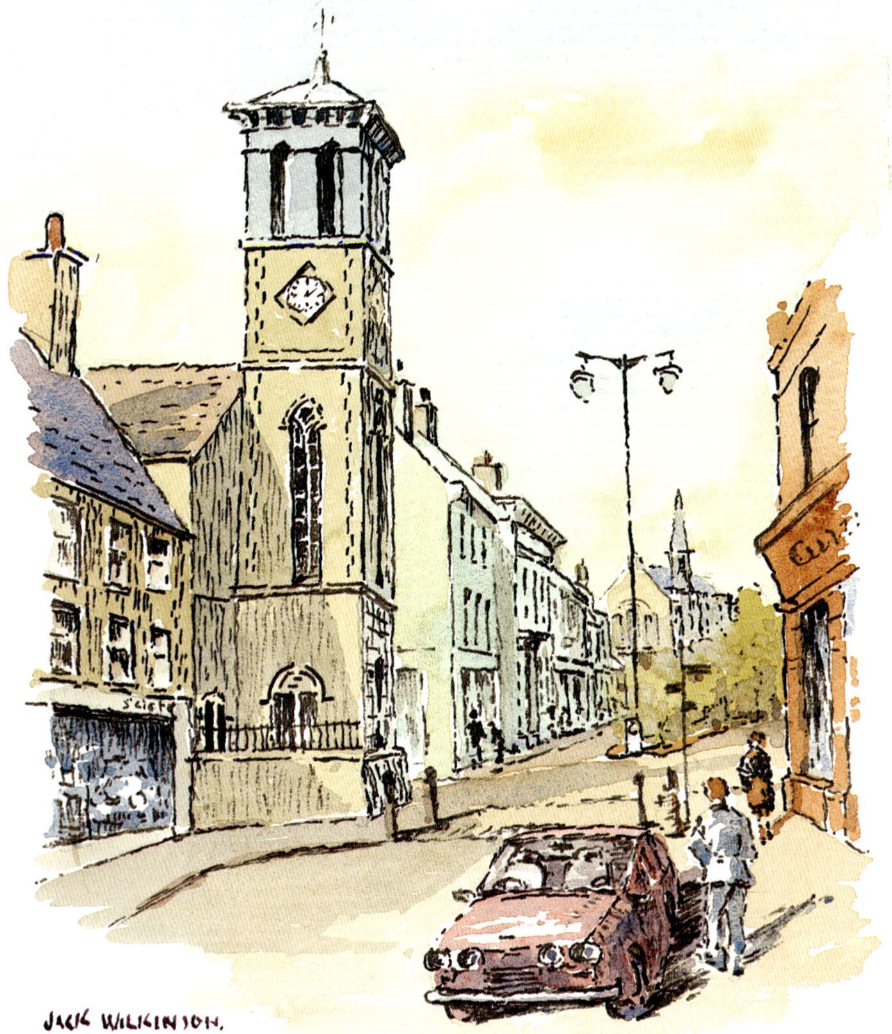
JACK WILKINSON.

O

Name and Address	*Telephone*

Main Street, Ballymoney

Main Street is the main commercial thoroughfare of the town and its oldest recognisable street. It leads up the hill to the town clock and the centre of the town where stands the building variously known as the Baronial Hall, the Market House, Court House, Old Town Hall and, since 1907, Masonic Hall. It was built by the Earl of Antrim around 1775 and from its tower in 1798 two United Irishmen were hanged. The magistrate responsible for passing the death sentence was Mr. George Hutchinson, known as 'Bloody Hutchinson' who lived in the Manor House and whose ghost is still said to haunt the street.

With thanks to Wilson McMichael

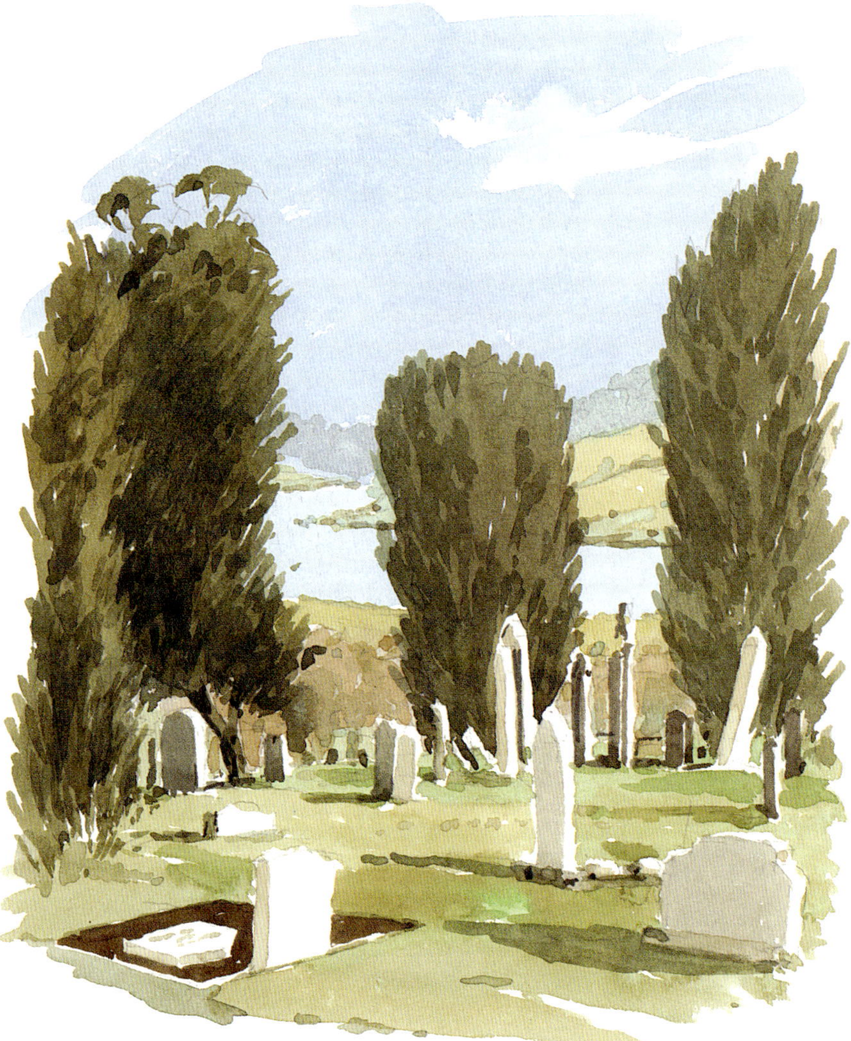
JACK WILKINSON

P

Name and Address	*Telephone*

Vow Old Graveyard

Vow Old Graveyard commands a beautiful view of the River Bann where a ferry once plied regularly. In the Middle Ages a church stood at the far end of the graveyard but no trace of it survives. In the Ulster Visitation Book of 1622 it was described as 'decayed'. As a place where people from Counties Antrim and Londonderry could easily meet, it was chosen as the spot for the ordination, in the open air, of the first minister of the Reformed Presbyterian (Covenanter) Church in Ireland. He was the Rev. William Martin and the ceremony took place on 2nd July 1757.

With thanks to Richard Dickson

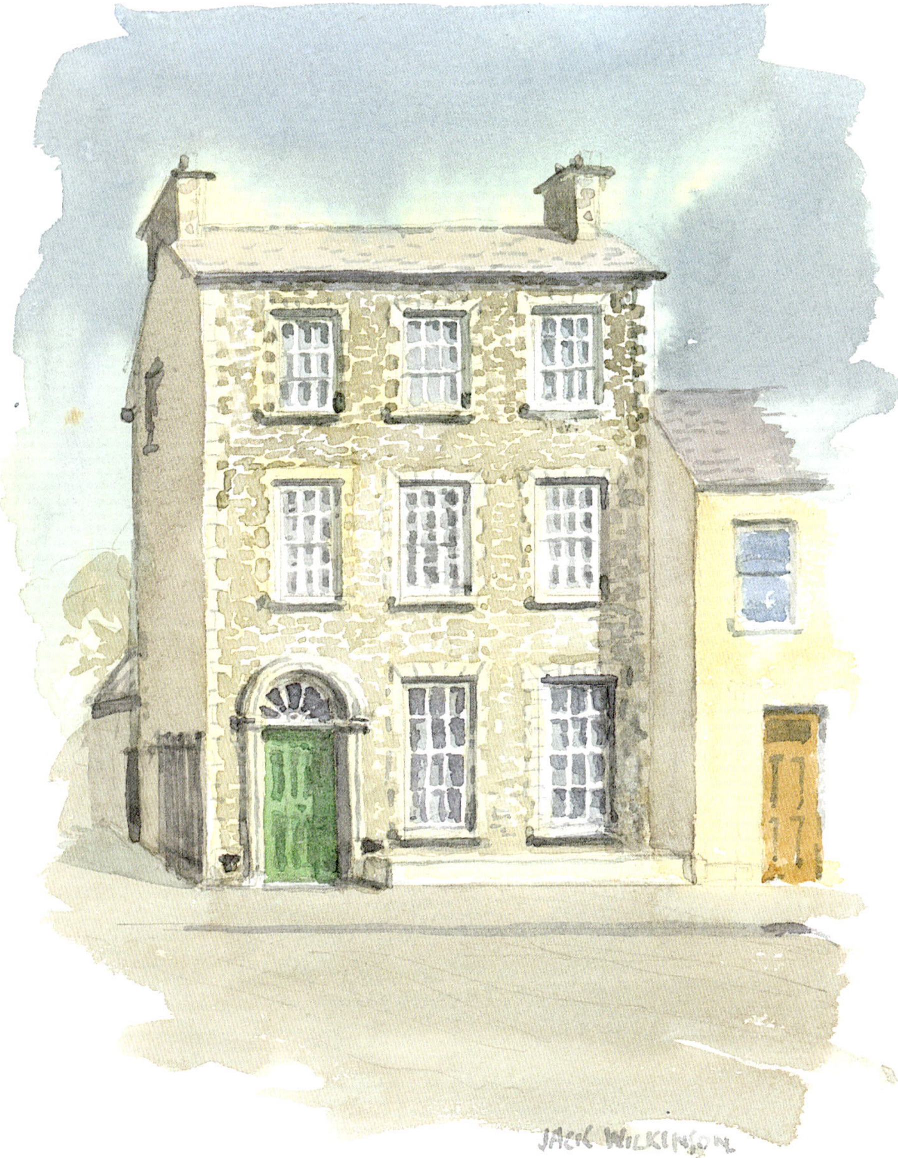
JACK WILKINSON

Q

Name and Address	*Telephone*

No. 16 Charlotte Street

A high and rather narrow Georgian house in Charlotte Street, Ballymoney, this building was originally much lower, as may still be seen in the stonework on its facade. It has good Georgian windows and a fine doorway which is unusually off-centre. The semi-circular fanlight above the door is typical of many Georgian houses. The house has lost its iron railings but it has its original foot scraper by the side of the door, a reminder of the days when the streets were often dirty. In 1832 the Ordnance Survey Memoir of Ballymoney noted that "the streets are not kept clean and in wet weather particularly it is unpleasant to walk through them."

With thanks to Insurance and Travel

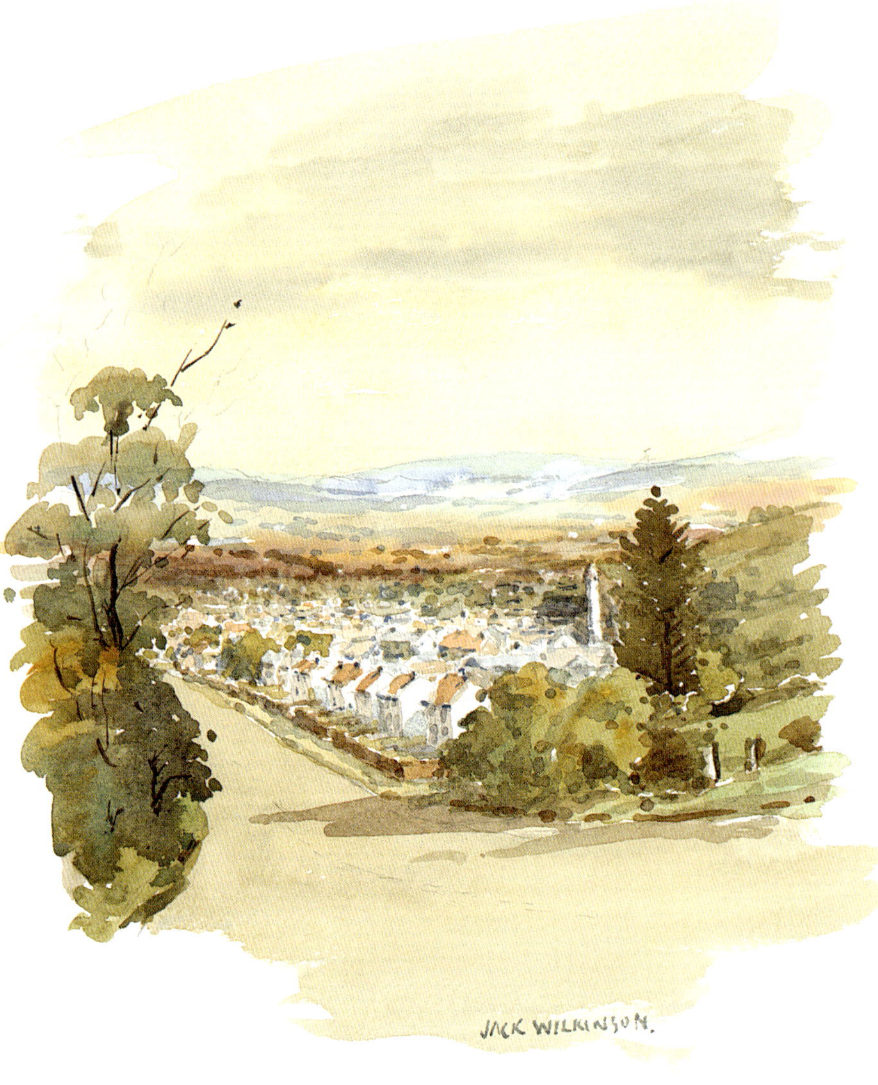
JACK WILKINSON.

R

Name and Address | *Telephone*

Dunloy Village

Dunloy means 'the fort of Lorus' or 'the fort of the hollow ground' and the fort concerned is most likely Carrowdoon in the hollow ground of Lower Dunloy. The village grew up where the old road from Ahoghill to Ballymoney was crossed by another road from the Bann to the coast. In 1814 it is described as the 'chief hamlet' of the parish of Finvoy and "the only one which bids fair to be a little town". It was much developed by George Hutchinson, its landlord, in the early decades of the 19th century but when the 'new line' was cut in the 1840s all his work was in vain as from then on little traffic passed through it.

With thanks to Dixons Contractors

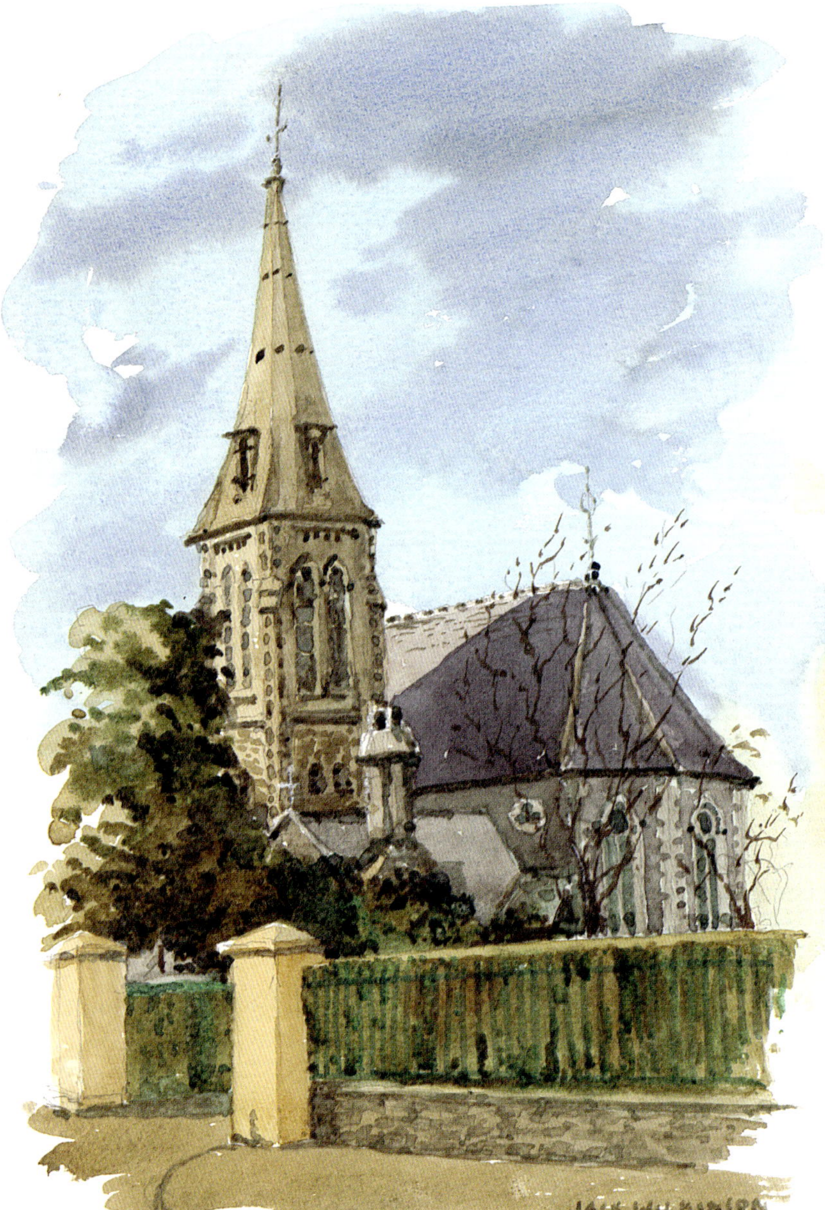
JACK WILKINSON

S

Name and Address	*Telephone*

ROMAN CATHOLIC CHURCH OF OUR LADY AND ST. PATRICK

The Roman Catholic Church of Our Lady and St. Patrick, Castle Street, was opened and dedicated on 2nd June 1878 and its erection was largely due to the work of the parish priest of the time, the Very Rev. John McErlane, who is buried in a vault beneath the main altar. The spire is one hundred and twenty feet high and it contains a bell inscribed "Me fieri fecit populus Catholicus de Ballymoney". The altars and pulpit are of Caen stone and were the work of the celebrated Dublin sculptors, Powell and Earley. The mosaic decoration on the ceiling above the altars and the six gilded seraphim were by another Dublin craftsman named Mannix and some of the glass is by Meyer of Munich.

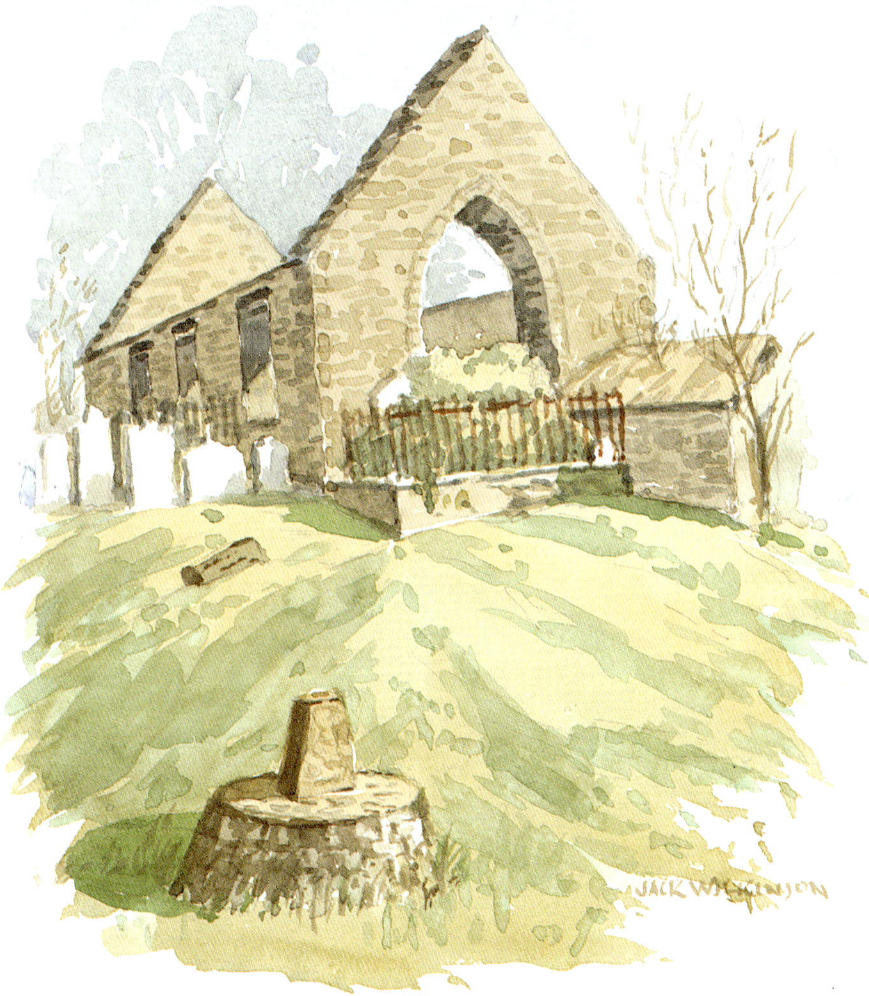

T

Name and Address	*Telephone*

Derrykeighan Old Church

Derrykeighan Old Church stands on a very ancient Christian site. A carved stone of an even earlier period was discovered in a corner of the ruins in 1981 and a replica is now mounted in the graveyard. The rectors of Derrykeighan in the 17th century were Prebendaries of Carncastle and most of them were absentees. The first Prebendary to officiate regularly in Derrykeighan was William Fullerton, appointed in 1628, whose tombstone is built into the north wall of the church. The church was in use until 1831 when a new church in Dervock was erected. Many parishioners did not want to leave the old site but a mysterious explosion made the old church unusable.

With thanks to Daniel Gillan Tower Bar

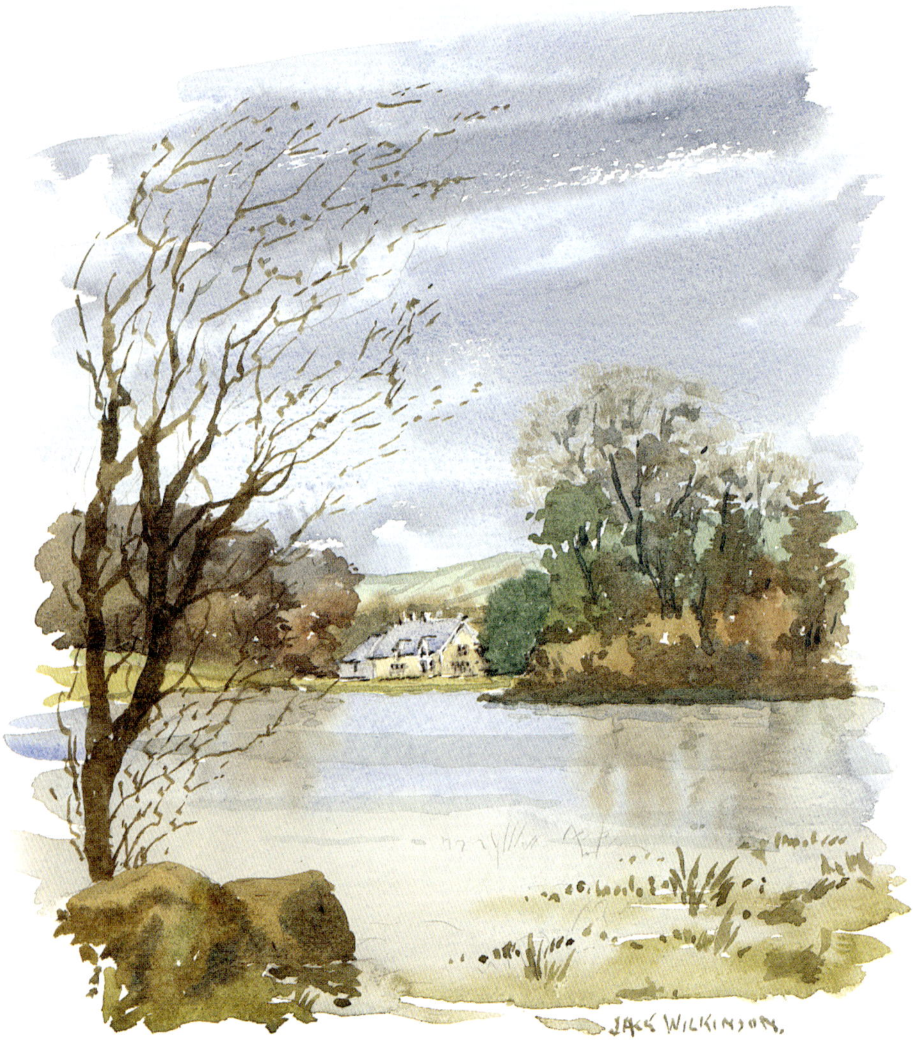
JACK WILKINSON.

U

Name and Address	*Telephone*

THE COTTAGE AND LAKE AT LISSANOURE

One of North Antrim's most beautiful scenes, Lough Giel gives its name to the townland and parish and has in it a crannog, a lake dwelling from Celtic times. The cottage was used as an occasional dwelling for the owners of the estate, the Macartney family, although it was also used as a house for the farm manager, or landsteward, or for spinster aunts. When their castle was destroyed by an accidental explosion of gunpowder on 5th October 1847, the Macartney family moved into permanent residence in the cottage. Nearby is the pleasure garden with two very old monkey puzzles and the ruined church of St. Mary by the Lake which contains the Macartney tombs.

With thanks to McAfee Properties

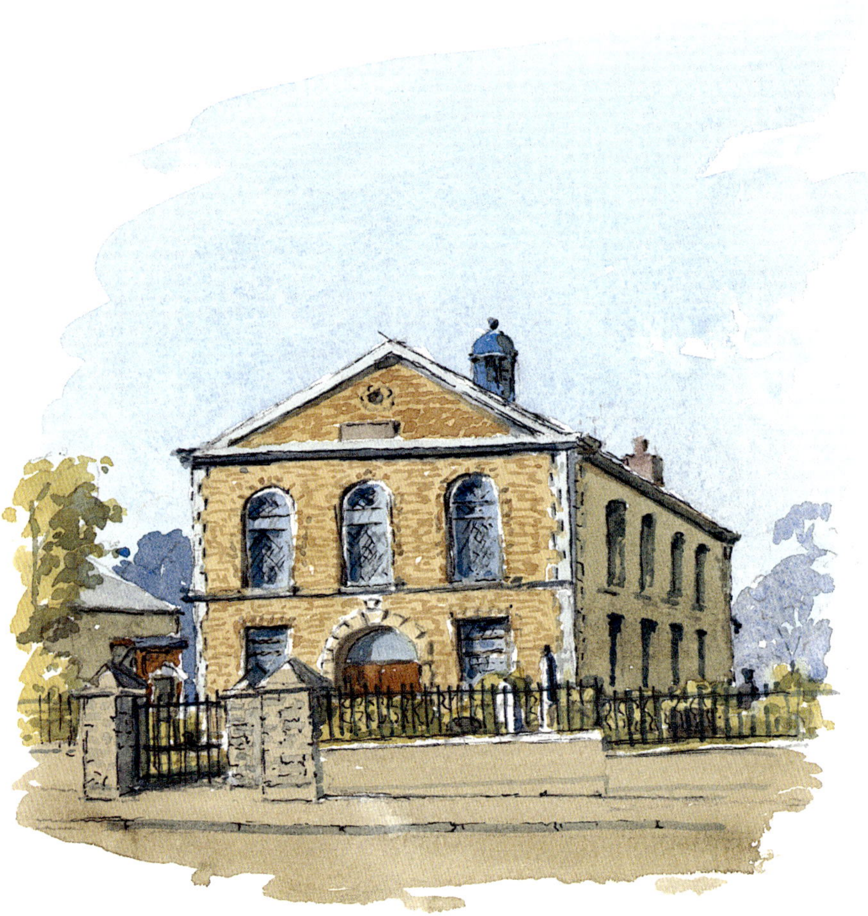

JACK WILKINSON.

V

Name and Address	*Telephone*

St. James's Presbyterian Church, Ballymoney

Built in black basalt with some architectural pretensions, especially its gable pediment above the entrance door, this fine example of a barn church was built in 1834 at the head of the town on the main road to Coleraine. When the new road was made in the 1840s the church was left in a cul-de-sac but the congregation has grown over the years and is now the largest of its denomination in the town. It is said that its name comes not from any dedication of the people to St. James but rather because that was the name of their first minister, the Rev. James Ussher. Other illustrious ministers have included the Rev. Dr. D.D. Boyle and the Very Rev. Dr. T.M. Johnston.

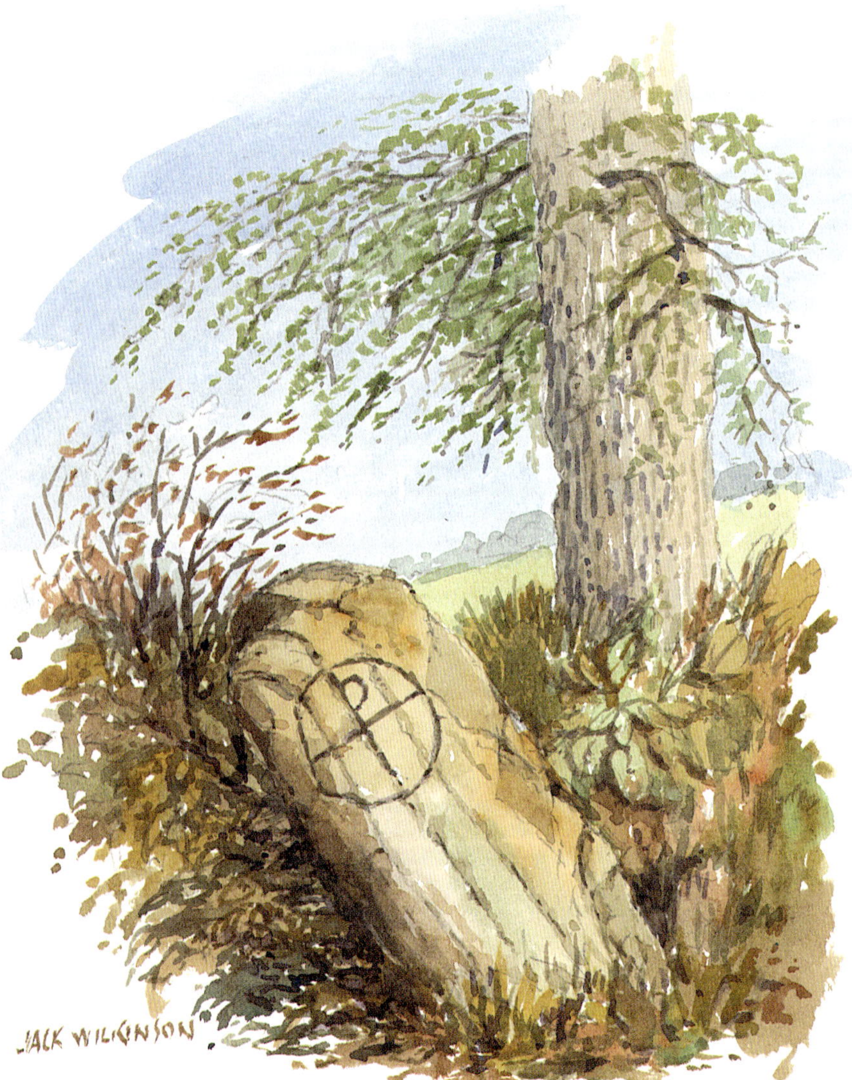
JACK WILKINSON

W

Name and Address	*Telephone*

CHI-RHO STONE, KILRAUGHTS

The Chi-Rho Stone at Drumaquern, Kilraughts, now stands on the side of an old disused laneway. Originally it stood in the adjacent field but was "sliped" to its present position at the beginning of this century. The chi and the rho, the first two letters of the name of Christ in Greek, are on the stone enclosed within a circle. This is unusual enough and links early Irish Christianity with European thought, but what is even more unusual is the fact that on the other side is to be found the same symbols but with the rho reversed. The stone is known as 'Old Patrick' and is believed in local tradition to commemorate a visit by the saint to the area.

With thanks to The Bookworm

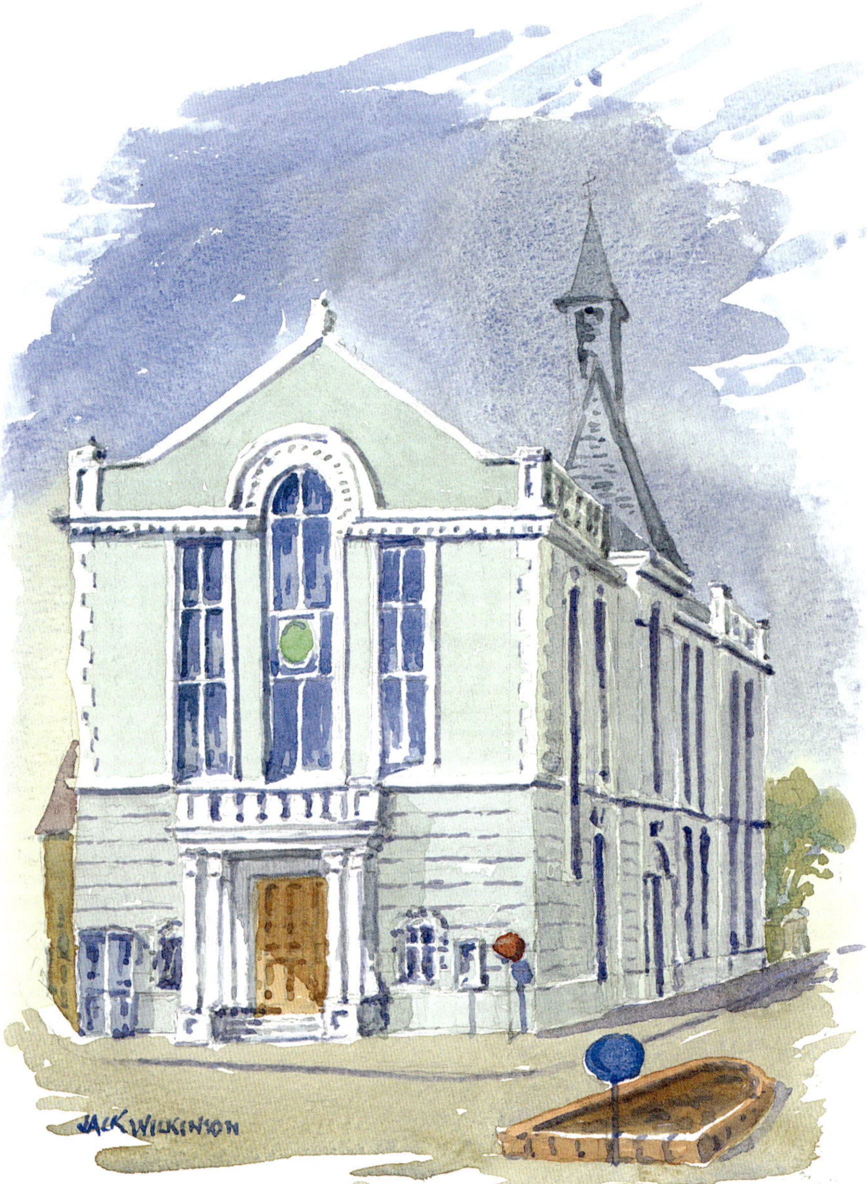
JACK WILKINSON

X

Name and Address	*Telephone*

Ballymoney Town Hall

Ballymoney Town Hall was built in 1866 with public subscriptions collected mostly by Dr. William Taylor and Mr. James Cramsie, whose large portraits hang in the main hall. In the minor hall are portraits of many notables of the town and district including William Orr, Thomas McElderry, Robert MacAfee, George Shiels, Mr. and Mrs. W.J. Megaw, Dr. S.B. Boyd, and Sir William McCleery. At the entrance is a bronze plaque to Kennedy K. McArthur of Dervock who won the Marathon Race in the 1912 Olympic Games and in the main corridor a bronze mural relief commemorates the playwright George Shiels.

With thanks to McIntyre Newsagents

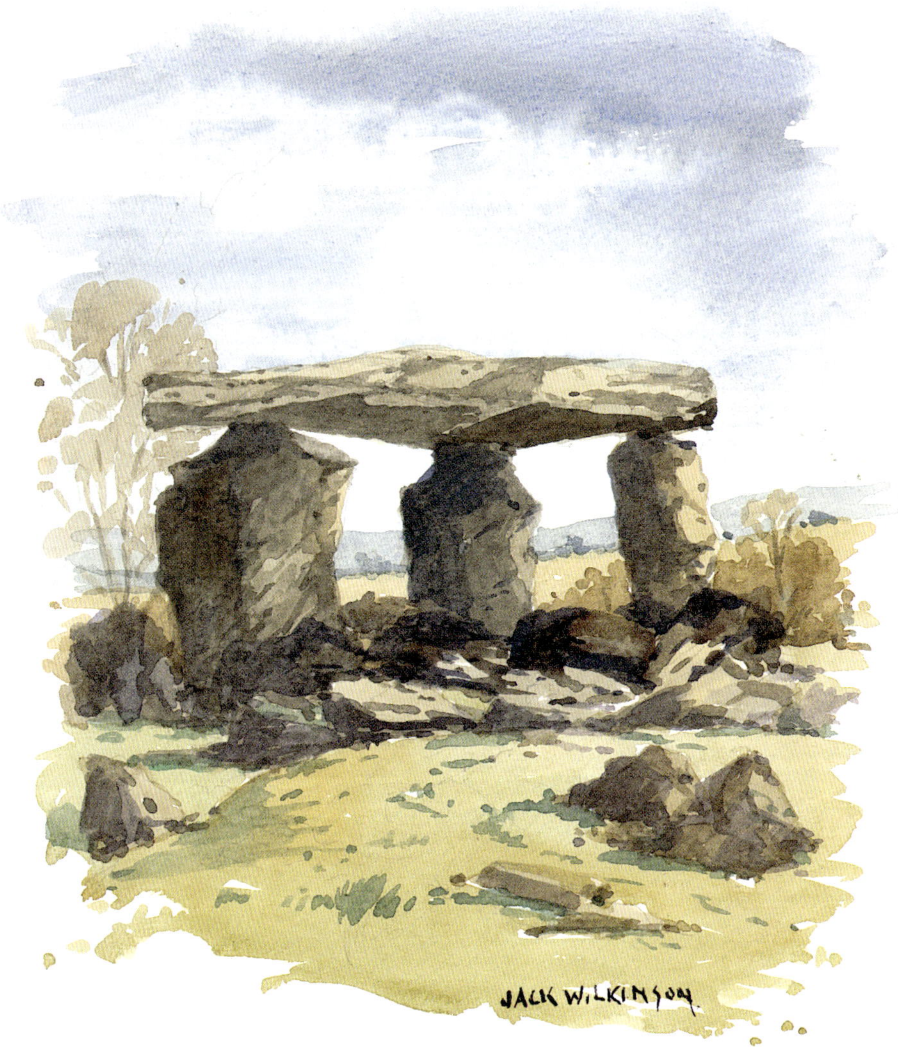
JACK WILKINSON

Y

Name and Address	*Telephone*

The Broad Stone, Finvoy

The Broad Stone, situated on the Craigs Mountain in the parish of Finvoy, is probably the remains of a cairn from the New Stone Age. It once had a circle of stones around it about forty five feet in diameter. There is a great cap stone raised originally on five other stones set edgewise as pillars. The rector of Finvoy, the Rev. James Grier recorded in 1814 that "the foremost supporters are still standing but some of the back ones have fallen and the cap stone has therefore sunk from its original horizontal level". Grier said there was a chamber below "deep enough for a middle-sized man to stand upright in" and this chamber connected with two other chambers which ran northward from it.

With thanks to The Art Shop

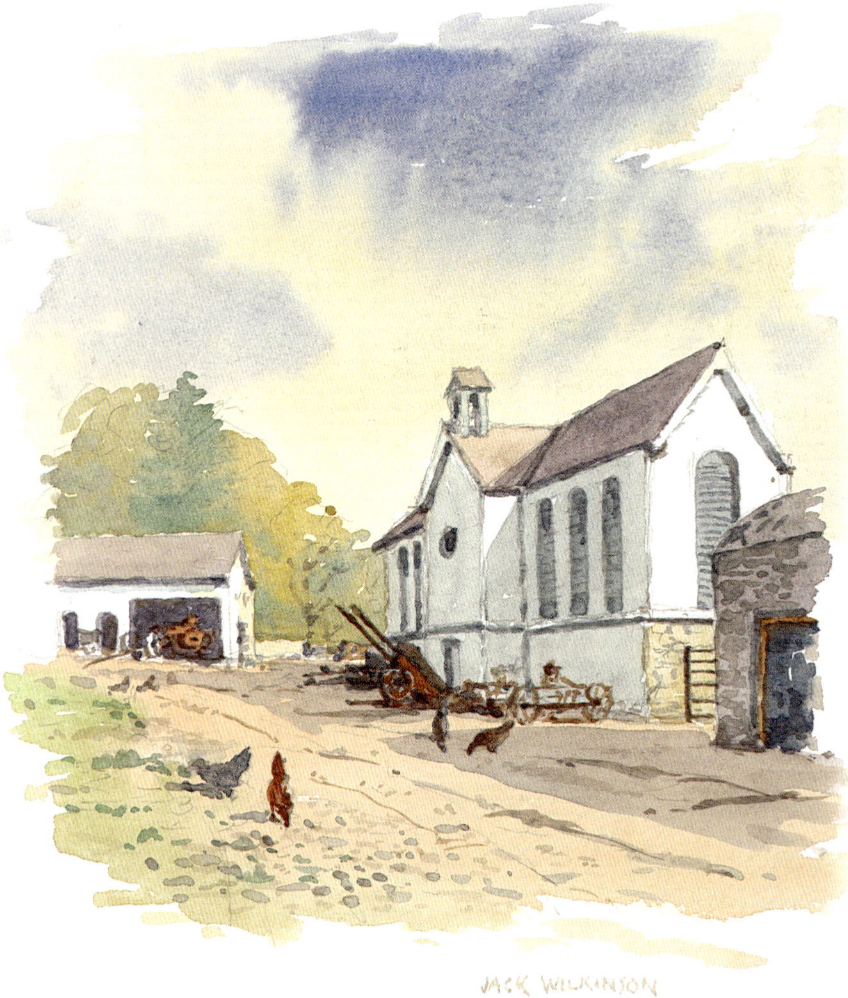
JACK WILKINSON

Z

Name and Address	*Telephone*

Leslie Hill

Leslie Hill, Ballymoney, was described as "unfinished and full of company" by Mrs. Delaney when she visited it in October 1758. The house was completed by James Leslie in 1760 and is three storeys high with a very fine fanlighted doorway. Originally there were one-storey pavilions at each side and these set off the house considerably. In the yard is a Bell Barn (seen here) described by Arthur Young in 1780 as "the best contrived I have seen in Ireland". Now a Heritage Farm, the buildings featured are largely 18th century and contain interesting collections of vehicles, implements and utensils used in farming over the last three centuries.

With thanks to Heritage Farm Park, Leslie Hill

Local Directory and Sponsors

We would like to take this opportunity to thank the following businesses and organisations without whose help and support this book would not have been possible.

Unless otherwise stated all addresses are in Ballymoney (Telephone code 012656)

Business Name and Address	Tel	Fax
Art Shop & Gallery & Framing		
The Art Shop		
1 Queen Street	65528	
Auctioneers & Property Agents		
McAfee Properties		
21 Main Street	67676	67666
32 New Road, Coleraine (01265)	42224	52666
Bank		
Northern Bank		
6 High Street	62225	66847
Bar		
The Village Inn		
1 Bellaghy Road, Dunloy	57447	
Book Shop		
The Bookworm		
19 Church Street	65614	65614
Builders Merchants		
J S C Builders Merchants		
20 Gracehill Road, Armoy (012657)	51811	51011
Building Contractor		
Dixons Contractors		
143 Tullaghans Road, Dunloy	57310	57310
Hairdressers – Unisex		
Top Ten		
66 Main Street	63539	
Health Store		
The Nature Nook		
4-6 Victoria Street	64178	64178
Heritage Farm Park		
Leslie Hill Heritage Farm Park, Leslie Hill	66803/63109	
Jeweller & Engraver		
Richard Dickson		
10 Victoria Street	62146	65233

Business Name and Address	Tel	Fax
Joinery and UPVC Products		
S. Dooey & Co.		
7 Presbytery Lane, Dunloy	57221	57464
Ladies Fashions		
The Winsome Lady		
76 Main Street	663585	
Local Government		
Ballymoney Borough Council		
Riada House, 14 Charles Street	62280	65150
Men's, School and Sports Wear		
Wilson McMichael		
4 High Street	62625	
Newsagent		
McIntyre		
5 High Street, Ballymoney	662168	
60 The Promenade, Portstewart (01265)	832788	834200
Public House		
Daniel Gillan Tower Bar		
41 Church Street	62431	
Restaurant & Wine Bar		
Gossoon's Wine Bar/Parklight Restaurant		
49 Main Street	67111	
Self Catering Accomodation		
Old Ballyness Cottages		
36 Castlecat Road, Bushmills (012657)	31252	
Solicitors		
Murphy Irwin & Co.		
5 Church Street	62132	62585
Travel Agent and Specialist Long Haul Travel Consultant		
Insurance & Travel		
25 Church Street	62277	
26-28 Kingsgate Street, Coleraine (01265)	42277	53421
49 The Promenade, Portstewart (01265)	832277	836636

Open Diary

This section is provided to record personal dates such as birthdays, anniversaries and other important annual events.

January

1

2

3

4

5

6

7

8

9

10

11

12

13

14

15

16

17

18

19

20

21

22

23

24

25

26

27

28

29

30

31

February

1

2

3

4

5

6

7

8

9

10

11

12

13

14

15

16

17

18

19

20

21

22

23

24

25

26

27

28

29

March

1

2

3

4

5

6

7

8

9

10

11

12

13

14

15

16

17

18

19

20

21

22

23

24

25

26

27

28

29

30

31

April

1

2

3

4

5

6

7

8

9

10

11

12

13

14

15

16

17

18

19

20

21

22

23

24

25

26

27

28

29

30

May

1

2

3

4

5

6

7

8

9

10

11

12

13

14

15

16

17

18

19

20

21

22

23

24

25

26

27

28

29

30

31

June

1

2

3

4

5

6

7

8

9

10

11

12

13

14

15

16

17

18

19

20

21

22

23

24

25

26

27

28

29

30

July

1

2

3

4

5

6

7

8

9

10

11

12

13

14

15

16

17

18

19

20

21

22

23

24

25

26

27

28

29

30

31

August

1

2

3

4

5

6

7

8

9

10

11

12

13

14

15

16

17

18

19

20

21

22

23

24

25

26

27

28

29

30

31

September

1

2

3

4

5

6

7

8

9

10

11

12

13

14

15

16

17

18

19

20

21

22

23

24

25

26

27

28

29

30

October

1

2

3

4

5

6

7

8

9

10

11

12

13

14

15

16

17

18

19

20

21

22

23

24

25

26

27

28

29

30

31

November

1
2
3
4
5
6
7
8
9
10
11
12
13
14
15
16
17
18
19
20
21
22
23
24
25
26
27
28
29
30

December

1

2

3

4

5

6

7

8

9

10

11

12

13

14

15

16

17

18

19

20

21

22

23

24

25

26

27

28

29

30

31

Cottage Publications

Dear Reader

We hope you have found this book both enjoyable and useful. If you feel that it could have been improved in any way do please let us know.

This book is one of our 'Illustrated History and Companion' range. Other towns and areas currently featured in this range include:–

Ballycastle and the Heart of the Glens
Ballymena
Bangor
City of Derry
Coleraine and the Causeway Coast
Donaghadee
Hillsborough
Holywood
Larne and the Road to the Glens
Newtownards

If you require more information call us on 01247 883876 or write to:–

Cottage Publications
15 Ballyhay Road
Donaghadee, Co. Down
N. Ireland
BT21 0NG

Timothy S Johnston